SOMETIMES THERAPY IS AWKWARD

A Collection of Life-Changing Insights for the Modern Clinician

NICOLE ARZT

CONTENTS

INTRODUCTION

Before I was a therapist or writer, I was a reader.

Growing up, I read everything—the backs of cereal boxes, shampoo labels, my mom's trashy romance books. I devoured newspaper articles and instruction manuals, and I lived for trips to the bookstore and local library.

As therapists, we know that reading is an integral part of our profession. I think most of us enjoy reading, and even those who don't like to pretend they do. After all, what therapist's office doesn't have rows of books on the shelf arranged just so? Did you purchase my bright-yellow paperback and imagine how and where you would position it in your office?

I have read so many books about this profession. A handful profoundly defined my identity as a therapist, but many of them felt dry, academic, and utterly disconnected from reality. If anything, reading those books often left me feeling even more insecure about my craft.

Therapists have good intentions when they write books. But their message often becomes diluted—it becomes less about the nuances of personal development as a therapist and more about showcasing a series of their successes. When therapists write books, they often describe nothing less than pure clinical wizardry. They share how a single intervention reversed years of complex trauma. They talk about how a simple cognitive reframe cured the contentious resentment between a couple headed toward divorce.

As a new therapist, I experienced their all-knowing insight as ingenious and their techniques nothing short of magical. But their effortless expertise also left me worried. Would I transform into a flawless therapist like them? Could I replicate their brilliance?

While they dreamt entirely new theories in their sleep, I was busy being awkward and overly sarcastic. I said "dude" and "fuck" in my sessions. I spent a great deal of time frantically looking up "interesting group activities" online. Furthermore, my therapy never seemed life-altering. I doubted myself and my abilities constantly.

And while those authors meditated between clients, I drank copious amounts of coffee and ruminated about my flopped interventions. I didn't have cures for my clients. I did, however, have constant thoughts along the lines of believing my neighbor's hamster would be a better therapist than me.

Was I a complete imposter? Was I just a naive child playing dress-up with my diplomas and discount Banana Republic outfits? Or could I effectively diagnose and treat mental illness like those expert therapists? I wasn't so sure. Sometimes, I'm still not sure.

I am a licensed marriage and family therapist. I've worked in various settings, including schools, hospitals, nonprofit centers, residential facilities, and private practice. But this is just one part of my identity. I'm also a woman, wife, mother, and avid believer in desserts and long hikes. In addition to my therapy career, I am a professional writer, and I own a content marketing agency specializing in helping therapists build their online presence. Finally, I am the founder of Psychotherapy Memes, a global community that acknowledges both the joys and struggles of being a therapist.

I didn't have a business plan or motive when I started Psychotherapy Memes in 2018. I just wanted to make and share memes. As it turned out, many people enjoyed those memes! More than anything, my community inspired me to write this book. At the time of this writing, we have over 65,000 Instagram followers, most of whom identify as mental health professionals.

The surprise success catapulted me into this strange role of a virtual social media influencer. I take this role seriously—I know that large platforms have the capacity to influence dynamic change and critical thought. Through my social media experience, I have gathered some basic assumptions about therapists:

- We often graduate from school feeling woefully unprepared.

- We're scared we won't make any money.

- We (mostly) love the work we do.

- We doubt ourselves constantly.

- We second-guess our career choice.

- We often feel unappreciated in the healthcare system.

- We're tired of subpar working conditions.

- We feel alone in our insecurities.

- We wonder if we're helping our clients.

- We have a dark sense of humor.

I want to note that I struggled immensely in writing this book. I don't have overly impressive credentials. I'm not an expert in theory, and I haven't published any world-famous research. While writing, I often lamented to my husband about my perceived incompetence. I doubted that I had anything real to offer prospective and current therapists. He encouraged me to keep writing. Everyone who knew I was writing this book encouraged me to keep writing. So, I kept writing.

I believe in the work we therapists do. We deserve to feel supported and empowered in this field. But we differ from our predecessors, and we need more books to reflect those differences. For instance, maybe we aren't as formal and poised as some seasoned therapists, but we are still empathic and dynamic. Maybe we feel torn between holding professional titles and being authentic humans. And maybe we're done with those clickbait articles telling us seven ways to improve our self-care.

I am not a psychotherapy expert. I continue to make many mistakes. I question my own mental health. At times, I struggle with immense shame and fear and self-doubt. But I wrote the book I wish I could have read when I was starting this career.

This book is for aspiring therapists, new therapists, and any therapist who identifies with feeling ashamed, afraid, and uncomfortable in their profession.

I see you. I am you. And I believe we need space for the messy and flawed and hopelessly insecure parts that can go along with doing this work.

ACKNOWLEDGMENTS

First, I want to acknowledge and thank all the many clients I have worked with over the years. Therapy is chilling soul work, and you continue to shape, challenge, and inspire me. You are so brave; please know I feel truly honored to have been a part of your life.

I want to acknowledge all the professors, mentors, supervisors, and colleagues I've had over the years. Some of you were supremely helpful in teaching me about what it meant to be a therapist. Some of you showed me exactly what not to do. Your feedback has stayed with me throughout my career.

Behind every successful therapist is another successful therapist who believes in them. I want to thank the therapists who have supported me in my personal growth. I am a better person because of the reflective work I continue to embrace.

I want to thank Kate Western, Maritza Mata, Michelle Liva, Lauren Landwerlin, Luis Figueroa, Nicole Dilella, Rebecca Hillman, Sonia Milbank, and Stephanie Grogan for reading and tearing apart my initial drafts and helping shape this book.

To all my Psychotherapy Memes fans and followers, you are so loyal and passionate about psychotherapy. You give me so much excitement for where our field is headed, and I love this community we have created. Thank you for believing in me.

To my family, thank you for always eagerly encouraging me to write. I suppose I really am a legitimate author now!

To my kindred spirit, thank you for being an unconditionally loving best friend. You know who you are, and you are amazing.

Jeremy, you are my partner, my confidant, and my genuine soul mate. In so many ways, we wrote this book together, bouncing around ideas whenever we had the chance. You always believe in me, and I love you endlessly. I still can't believe you're my husband. In the words of my brother, may we continue to love and analyze each other for the rest of our lives.

Bryson, I started writing this book just after you were born. I drafted many of these pages during your naps, and I often felt selfish for working while you were so young. That said, I hope I can model the importance of balance, hard work, and passion to you. You made me a mom, and you make me a better woman. You are perfect. I love you infinitely, and I am sorry your parents are both therapists.

CHAPTER 1:

(ALMOST) EVERYTHING I BELIEVED ABOUT THERAPISTS WAS WRONG

Throughout my editing process, I changed this book title several times. I reexamined one title, *Reassurance for the Growing Therapist*, after two people suggested that it clashed with my raw and controversial content.

I suppose the reassurance is secondary. I do hope that you finish this book feeling more reassured and confident in your practice. But this isn't just a book about reassurance. It's a book that highlights the awkward nuances of psychotherapy and normalizes some of the insecurities and fears most of us face.

This book chronicles the stuff nobody told me. It's the stuff that invariably defines therapy, but it's also the stuff that doesn't always have a name or term. I am a therapist who entered this field without really knowing what being a therapist meant. Here are some lessons I've learned along the way.

Myth: Successful Therapists Don't Feel Insecure

My first supervisor enchanted me. As a trainee, she wore wisdom and poise like fitted suits. In supervision, she talked without hesitation. A child who wouldn't speak? Try this play therapy intervention. A couple reeling from infidelity? Explore their thoughts about this specific fear. I knew about diagnosing and assessing for suicide— she knew about solving the unsolvable mysteries of the human experience.

She spoke about therapy fiercely, and she never seemed baffled by a supervisee's question. She answered without pausing, gave suggestions as if she inherently always knew the best response. She was the epitome of intelligence.

But as much as I admired her confidence, it also intimidated me. Would I ever seem so effortless, so put-together, so *smart*? One day, after discussing how lost I felt with a new client, I shared how much I second-guessed myself, how much I doubted that I was really helping my clients. She smiled at me— her warm, nurturing smile, the kind that I knew made her clients feel secure and special. And then she said, "Your insecurities show you care. Nobody needs you to have all the answers. People need to know you care."

Your insecurities show you care.

She wasn't wrong. I cared about my clients deeply. I cared without limitations, without remorse. New therapists are so hungry, but they don't know how to cook. They forage and eat whatever scraps are available. New therapists are the most fragile species, but I'd argue they care the most.

Her response didn't change my self-doubt. It just made me more aware of its needed place in my training. Eventually, I felt less shackled by my perceived incompetence. But years later, her words stay with me.

I now know that almost all therapists doubt themselves. And they should. Therapy penetrates the most tender and raw pieces of the human soul. It weaves and unwinds and stitches and attacks both the client and the therapist. It's convoluted work, and I think many of us forget that in our quest to be perfect.

When we're humble, we're more empathic and understanding, and we don't assume we know all the answers. Instead, we remain open to learning and growing. As therapists, this curiosity is one of our greatest assets.

Myth: Therapists Are Healthy and Well-Adjusted Professionals

I've known therapists who have slept with clients, who have self-medicated with marijuana and prescription pills before every single session, who have billed for treatment fraudulently, and who have lied about their credentials.

Yet, I once believed therapists embodied optimal mental health. I know that many clients also believe this myth, and some therapists do as well. Since we're technically experts in mental health, we may assume we represent complete emotional stability.

Paradoxically, we are attracted to pain. We spend our days hanging out with people who have serious problems, people with trauma and depression and resentment. We hold on to the inexplicable terrors plaguing humanity. We listen to the treacherous secrets our clients refuse to tell anyone else. Likewise, while doing this work, we bring our stories, pains, and fears into each session. And through treating the problems of others, some therapists strategically avoid examining their own.

We might be experts in mental health, but our expertise doesn't fix our own problems. Some therapists will do the necessary emotional work to better themselves. These therapists will continue to evolve in their personal growth—and their professional growth will likely follow. Others, however, will continue to fall short because of their shortcomings.

Myth: Successful Therapists Always Know What to Do with Their Clients

In my first year of training, I worked with a thirty-something woman. She felt stressed at her job—her boss was tyrannical, the hours were crazy, and she described feeling deeply unfulfilled during the nine or ten hours she spent in her office cubicle each day. Her fiancé had empathized with her struggles. He had encouraged her to quit and finish her college degree; he had insisted he made enough money to support the two of them while she figured out her next move.

One Friday morning, they ate bagels for breakfast and reviewed their weekend plans for meeting with their wedding photographer. He asked if she wanted salmon for dinner. He told her to take his car because he wanted to get an oil change for hers. She thanked him and kissed him quickly—she was running late. On his way to get the oil change, another car ran a red light, and my client's fiancé died on impact.

There's crying. There's crying in therapy. And then there's gut-wrenching crying, the kind that leaves you flailing on the floor, cursing at your god, feeling hopeless and directionless as you plead to wake up from this impossible nightmare.

My client was inconsolable, and I didn't know what to do to help her. I listened. I held space. I allowed her to feel. But my efforts felt like tiny water droplets in the middle of the ocean. I couldn't fix her pain. I couldn't bring him back.

Successful therapists don't always know what to do. Our clients rock our worlds, and our uncertainties reflect that. Today, sitting with someone's deep pain no longer debilitates me in the ways it once did. Does it still hurt? Absolutely. It can hurt so much. However, I recognize that we can't always fix the hurt. I now know that most therapists recognize it's impossible to always know the next move or intervention or phrase.

We all struggle with immense doubt. Successful therapists learn to embrace it.

Myth: Therapists Give Advice

Advice isn't in limited supply. We have endless self-help books, blog posts, and inspirational quotes offering advice. Some of it is thought-provoking; most of it is one-dimensional and useless. Many times, our clients know what to do in a given situation. Therapists help explore the barriers that lie between knowing and doing.

Sometimes, we think we know what is best for our clients. Sometimes, we think the right answer is painfully obvious. One client drinks too much—he should quit. Another client hates her boyfriend—she should leave.

But if problems were this simplistic, if life existed on an obvious black-and-white plane, why have any need for therapy at all? Wouldn't a single session fix the client? Wouldn't a few clichéd lines of advice cure the issue?

It isn't our job to tell our clients what to do or how to do it. For one, that method assumes we have all the right answers (and we don't). Moreover, it assumes that our clients have the willingness, capacity, or motivation to make and maintain those changes.

Our job is to provide support and compassion. We support people in finding their conclusions about how they want to live their lives. We don't force them on to our preferred paths.

Myth: Therapists Don't Make Any Real Money

During my first paid internship, my younger brother worked part-time at Starbucks. I earned fifty cents an hour more than he did. I had a graduate degree; at the time, he only had his high school diploma. My colleagues told me I was lucky to make anything at all.

Therapists are among the lowest-paid professionals with graduate degrees. While I find this statistic appalling, many therapists seem to embrace this dreadful fate: *I wouldn't go into this field for the money. You need to live in a two-income household if you want to be a therapist. You should be a therapist because you want to help people—not because you want to chase a salary.*

I emphatically disagree with these harmful myths. I like being a therapist, and I like earning a good living. They can mutually exist. We are trained healthcare professionals. We can and should ask for what we're worth, raise our rates, and advocate for higher salaries. Additionally, our career has limitless opportunities, and we can take advantage of that flexibility. We can provide therapy, but we can do so much more. We can teach, mentor, write, supervise, manage, and conduct research. We can run our own private or group practices. We can host workshops and seminars, online classes, and conferences.

I also know that our beliefs about earning money often determine our earning potential. What messages do you tell yourself about therapists' salaries? Do you feel guilty for wanting to make more money? Do you believe you're supposed to be earning pennies? That you're supposed to do this work only from love and the desire to help?

If so, you probably won't earn much. You might, however, perpetuate a damaging stigma about therapists and increase your own chances of burnout and resentment.

Myth: One Credential Is Better Than Another Credential

Mental health professionals love to play this useless comparison game. Some therapists believe one combination of letters after a last name is superior over another. Then they sit on their licensed thrones and act like their way is the right way.

There isn't a universally best credential, but there probably is a best credential for *you*. I can't tell you whether you should become a psychologist or marriage and family therapist or school counselor. I can only tell you that different credentials offer different levels of focus and expertise. Some locations have specific preferences, and some agencies prefer to hire employees with certain credentials. You must determine which schooling, licensing, or credentials best support your goals. Ask questions, read, seek mentorship, and don't rush your decision. Nobody can do this research for you.

Keep in mind there isn't a right or wrong path. We need people who focus on microsystems, and we need people who focus on macrosystems. We need people who prescribe medication and people who prescribe meditation. Nobody is better or worse than anyone else. We all have a relevant place in the mental health sector.

Myth: Most Clients Are Ready To Change

As a client, I once spent about twenty minutes detailing every single problem I had with an ex-boyfriend. I hated his lies, his drawn-out apologies for the lies, his lack of ambition, and his apologies over his lack of ambition.

The venting felt cathartic, and my kind therapist listened with her hands folded neatly over her crossed legs. I then asked her what I should do next. She shrugged and told me that I had three choices: stay in the relationship and do nothing, stay in the relationship and work on changing myself, or leave. I glared at her and asked, "But what about everything I just told you? I'm not the one who needs to change!"

Like me, most clients want to change other people. They want to fix their mother's neediness or their boss's micromanaging or their neighbor's third cousin's bad breath. Subsequently, they also want to change their circumstances. They want a new house, a better job, or a smaller nose. They want to wake up into their perfect lives, but not if achieving such perfection requires work.

Like us, our clients struggle to look inward. It feels uncomfortable and exposing, and it's challenging work! As a result, we'll watch them deny and rationalize and suppress their feelings. We'll observe them as they take five steps forward and seventeen back. We'll become frustrated and impatient, and we'll also wonder if it's because we're not doing enough. We'll often forget that growth doesn't happen in linear directions.

Clients do want to change. But many obstacles make that change incredibly challenging.

Myth: Therapists Make Great Partners, Parents, and Friends

People love that my husband and I are both therapists. The dynamic fascinates them. They wonder, *Do you two analyze each other all day? Are you both super patient with each other? Do you always use your I-statements when you argue?*

In a short answer, absolutely not. In a long answer, I can be horrifically impatient, jaded, and judgmental. I can also be passive, passive-aggressive, and downright immature. It's quite a healthy combination, isn't it?

Now that we have a son, people constantly tell us how lucky he is to have us! I laugh at them. Can you imagine having two therapists as parents?

Like most therapists, I often hold my loved ones to different standards than my clients. At times, the energy spent being compassionate at work has left me feeling depleted at home. It is an unfortunate reality that few therapists discuss.

Likewise, I have (shockingly) learned that my family and friends don't share my same emotional depth. Some even use my career against me. Have you ever heard the phrase "Don't therapize me?" Even when I try to model healthy communication or vulnerability, it doesn't mean others react positively.

Therapists are humans. We get upset and flustered; we act irrationally, and we don't always think clearly. And because we give so much to our clients all day, we often have little to give to the rest of the world.

Myth: Therapy Must Be Face-to-Face to Be Effective

As this book reaches its final editing stages, America is in the throes of the horrific COVID-19 pandemic. To comply with social distancing and safety measures, many therapists are now providing telehealth services to their clients via video rooms or phone calls.

I share this myth because times change, and people change. And therapy and treatment have changed. What was relevant twenty years ago might be extinct today. Sigmund Freud, the father of psychoanalysis, deemed cocaine as a miracle drug. He wrote a famous paper that praised the magical benefits of cocaine. American physicians performed lobotomies until 1967. Until 2010, American insurance companies could deny people healthcare coverage based on preexisting mental illness. We don't always know what we don't know. We only grow and get better with time.

Therapy will evolve, and face-to-face therapy isn't the only answer. We must be open to new ways of helping. We may not agree with such changes, but we must promote diversity and flexibility in this profession. If we don't adapt, the career we love will die.

CHAPTER 2:

HOW TO COPE WITH YOUR EXCRUCIATING INSECURITIES

This is not intended to be one of those best-selling books about defying social norms and harnessing your most authentic, badass therapist self. I can't write that book because I rarely feel like a badass. Instead, I question my competence about eighty-three times a day. I can't walk without tripping over something, and I can't eat a meal without half the food getting on my shirt, face, or both. I frequently stumble over words with clients, use the wrong name, or forget what I'm about to say altogether. I often feel like I'm about twelve years old, but society considers me as an adult.

I know I'm not alone in these struggles. Every week, I facilitate a Q&A on the Psychotherapy Memes Instagram. I receive many questions from followers, but the most common ones include:

- How do I feel less anxious about starting my practicum or internship?

- How do I know if I'm a good therapist?

- When will I start feeling more confident as a therapist?

- What if this job isn't for me?

- What if I don't know what I'm doing with my clients?

Do you recognize this script? The one where a client reveals something, and you think: *Am I really supposed to be a therapist?! Because I think my dog, who still poops on the carpet (despite me paying for that expensive trainer who spat whenever he talked) could do a better job at comforting this person than me. I am terrible and useless. Maybe I should become a dog trainer. But even my own dog won't listen to me. I should have gotten a cat. Maybe it's not too late.*

First, dogs are always the superior choice over cats. Second, I know many of us doubt our abilities and competence. I also believe many of us desire validation—we want to know that our work is effective and meaningful.

My teachers and my favorite books helped me to feel reassured that my insecurities were perfectly normal. But it still never felt normal—it always felt like everyone else had something that I didn't.

Identify the Type of Insecure Therapist You Are

We experience insecurity for different reasons. These reasons have to do with our mental health and personalities. In examining and studying our field over the years, I've narrowed down these kinds of insecurities into four distinct categories. I believe understanding our type of insecurity can help us recognize our patterns—through this insight, we can learn to identify what we need to most work on improving.

#1: The Insecure Person

You aren't just insecure as a therapist. You're insecure because you exist. Maybe this insecurity comes from a deep place of depression, anxiety, or trauma. Perhaps it comes from your own struggles with low self-esteem. Either way, as a result, you often feel incapable with clients, and you also feel convinced they could benefit more from another therapist. You're regularly on the brink of crying, quitting, or signing up for some shady guru's $5,000 online self-help course. This therapist often:

- struggles with an anxiety disorder.

- requires ongoing reassurance and validation for their skills.

- questions their abilities while in session constantly.

- fantasizes about switching careers.

- feels untethered in their sessions (they obsessively study new interventions or read new books or sign up for new training courses with the hopes of building more confidence).

#2: The Perfectionist

Star student? Yep. Top athlete? Absolutely! Best therapist? That's the goal.

You might be high-achieving, but these accomplishments come at a high price. You must work tirelessly to maintain your perfectionism. Any perceived failure triggers a cataclysmic eruption of shame. As a therapist, you may desperately seek to control your clients' successes. Unexpected changes in your routine overwhelm you, and you associate "going with the flow" as a catchphrase for lazy people. You feel immense pressure to succeed because you don't believe you have inherent worth. Instead, you must earn this worth through external achievements. This therapist often:

- believes they will fail at anything they try.

- avoids taking risks or trying new things due to this unwavering fear of failure.

- wants to quantify abstract problems or solutions.

- obsesses over policies, procedures, and rules.

- puts too much on their plate and typically overworks.

- feels frustrated when clients don't succeed in predictable patterns.

#3: The Unresolved Life Shit Therapist

Your personal life is in absolute shambles, and your emotions seem erratic and catastrophic. Every client seemingly triggers you. You over-identify with their stories, and you hear yourself telling clients to do what you know *you* should be doing. Sometimes, you wonder if your clients are mentally healthier than you are. While all therapists have varying degrees of baggage, the unresolved life shit therapist hasn't worked through their distress. Therefore, they constantly struggle with themselves and with their clients. This therapist often:

- struggles with remaining objective in sessions.

- experiences intense and possibly uncontrollable countertransference.

- stresses over their own mental health.

- feels unable to maintain consistent and healthy boundaries with clients.

#4: The Straight-Up People Pleaser

You entered this field because you're a compassionate saint. Everyone knows you as empathic and patient. You bake cupcakes for coworkers' birthdays, and you always offer to cover that awful group everyone hates. Although you may feel exhausted by your incessant generosity, you don't know how to change. In your world, it's better to keep the peace than cause problems. The straight-up people pleaser often:

- struggles or avoids confrontation with clients.

- feels terrified and upset by aggressive clients.

- dreads all forms of feedback.

- feels paralyzed when faced with any semblance of conflict.

- tiptoes around delicate issues in sessions or the workplace.

Can You Be All of the Above (And, If So, Are You Screwed)?

Of course, you can have a variety of insecurities from among the different categories listed above. Most of us do. But no, you're not screwed. You're just a human, and you have weaknesses. Now you're more aware of what they are and how they impact your work and your clients. So, how do you actually deal?

Get Your Own Therapy

I once worked with a colleague who insisted he didn't need his own therapy. He felt so proud of his lack of mental health issues, and he reasoned that brain surgeons didn't need histories of personal brain surgeries to treat others effectively.

He wasn't entirely wrong. Therapists can apply evidence-based care and follow a prescribed model of treatment to their clients. We can identify a problem and use viable solutions to fix the problem. But we are not surgeons, and therapy is not brain surgery. Therapy has never been an exact science. The heart of what we do entails an abstract human element. We can have all the knowledge and skills, but we can't remove the human parts of our work.

Since we are very much human, we arrive at each session with feelings, biases, and expectations. Regardless of how stoic or logical we aspire to be, our individual self invariably bleeds into our work with clients. Since this self bleeds, we need it to be healthy. While personal therapy isn't the only way to cultivate mental health, what kind of therapists are we if we lack the willingness to pursue that option?

Behind every successful therapist is another therapist supporting them.

We all need therapy. Me, you, your supervisor, your professor, your favorite master therapist, and your colleague who microwaves fish in the communal microwave every lunch. Therapy makes us better therapists, and it also makes us better people. Therapy allows us to explore both our personal and professional lives in one space. It offers a valuable opportunity for growth, self-awareness, and healing.

We cannot fully support our clients without thoughtful insight into our own lives. Furthermore, how can we expect people to be honest and vulnerable with us if we never sit on the couch ourselves?

... But What If I've Already Tried Therapy, and It Didn't Work?

Even when they know it's important, many therapists love to resist personal therapy. Usually, we fear exposing our vulnerabilities. Sharing weakness with another professional might reinforce our sense of incompetence. What if they judge us? What if they question our abilities in this field? What if they pity our clients?!

Of course, we also assume therapists can't help us. I know that I have fallen into this hazardous trap many times. I tell myself I'm a mental health expert, that I know how to treat my problems. Therapists can't use their psychological sorcery on me—I recognize all their tricks and secrets!

I've also fired multiple therapists. One psychologist recommended I learn how to cook—he believed cooking would enrich all areas of my life. At the time, I was young and eager to please. I listened to his odd suggestion, and I attempted to make spaghetti instead of deal with my actual issues. I almost burned down my kitchen, and my problems didn't still improve. Another therapist suggested I color when I felt anxious. She insisted that it was "scientifically impossible" for the brain to experience anxiety while engaging in creative activity. I didn't color, and I didn't go back to her. I also met with a therapist who disregarded many boundaries—including, at one point, hiring me to work for her—before I understood the extent of her unethical actions.

Despite these awful experiences, I've also had fantastic therapy. I've learned about shame, my struggles with boundaries, my issues with control and perfectionism. I've processed traumas and family dynamics and my fears of unlovability. Just because I work in this field doesn't mean I'm above getting help for myself. I am not better or smarter than my clients. I just understand how some tools work. Where therapists have more insight than the average client, I also believe we tend to have more defense mechanisms.

Many people have asked me, "How do I find a therapist as a therapist?!" If you want the easy answer, I don't have it. There is no easy answer. Our profession doesn't make us inherently unique as people; it just makes us privy to how psychotherapy works. We find a good therapist the same way we find a good dentist or hairstylist or spouse. We ask friends and family for recommendations; we search online; we understand that, like everything in life, finding the right match sometimes requires a rigorous process of trial and error.

Learn to Accept the Abstract

When a light turns on in my car, I take it to my mechanic. He assesses the damage and fixes whatever I inevitably broke. When I clog the shower drain with all my tangled hair, I first have my husband try to fix it ten times, and then we call the plumber to unclog it. When I hand over a pile of (usually crumpled) paperwork to my accountant, he crunches the numbers and gives me my tax return.

I'm not suggesting any two professionals work the same. That assumption is faulty and even demeaning. Of course, all mechanics, plumbers, and accountants have different specialties and individual ways of doing things. But some careers have more precise objectives than others. The services are relatively straightforward. As consumers, we can expect to pay for a fairly predictable outcome.

As therapists, we don't have one of those careers. We usually can't offer tangible results to a client. We can't give them a new transmission or clean shower drain or tax return. We can't even give them an accurate estimate of the overall time or cost therapy requires. The abstract nature of therapy can frustrate both clients and therapists alike. How do we measure our clients' progress? How can we appropriately assess our own successes or failures? Finally, how do we cope with all these unknowns? Yet, accepting the abstract means accepting the following:

- We never really know who's walking into our office.

- We still don't know a lot about mental health.

- Most experts disagree on the "best way" to do therapy.

- Sessions rarely go according to plan.

- We may not know how much we really help our clients.

Most of us struggle with accepting the abstract. We think we need to have a clear understanding of our clients at all times. We might assume that uncertainty in our sessions indicates something is wrong. We don't make room for the unknown variables, for the loose and evolving here-and-now.

Learn to Accept Distractions

Client: "My mom pissed me off yesterday."

Me (thinking to myself): *Are we really going to talk about her mother again? Oh well, it's probably important. I know she's trying to set boundaries with her family.*

Damn, I have a bunch of lint on my pants. Will she notice if I brush it off? Does she see the lint? Why do I even bother with black pants when I have two white dogs? Why didn't I use my lint roller this morning? Where the hell is my lint roller?

Okay, back to focusing. But why is this room so warm? God, I'm literally sweating. Is she warm, too? Should I interrupt politely to ask?

STOP!

The temperature isn't bothering her. She needs you to listen to her. We obviously must address her mother's insufferable narcissism. But is her mother actually a narcissist? Or does she blame her mother for every inconsequential thing that ever went wrong in her life?

We should also probably talk about her depression. But during our last session, she said she wasn't feeling depressed. Am I supposed to prod at that more? She does have a tendency to mask her emotions. What if she's really depressed and does something drastic, and I didn't assess properly?

Oh God, this heat is making me thirsty. Ugh. Why did I leave my water bottle on my desk? And what should I eat for lunch today? Do I want a burrito? That might be too heavy. Maybe I'll go for a lettuce wrap.

Wait, I didn't listen to a thing she just said, and now she's crying. Shit!!

Daniel Wegner, Ph.D., an expert in thought-suppression research, conducted a well-known study where he asked his research participants to express their stream of consciousness for five minutes. During this exercise, he asked them to avoid thinking about a white bear. However, if the white bear came to mind, he instructed them to ring a bell. On average, they rang that bell about once per minute.

In another experiment, Wegner had the same set of participants complete a similar exercise. However, this time he explicitly instructed them to think of the white bear. As expected, they thought about the bear frequently. In fact, they thought about the bear more often than another group of participants who had been instructed to think about the white bear from the very beginning.

Today, this phenomenon is known as the *ironic process theory*. When we try to suppress a thought, another part of our brain checks in to ensure we're not thinking about it. Yet, this brain activity triggers us to think about it more.

Intrusive thoughts happen all the time. We think about our lint rollers and water bottles and our upcoming lunch plans. We feel agitated over a fight with our spouse, so we picture screaming in our client's face. Another client mentions how they bought a new bed, and we start thinking about the rest of their home's interior layout. Someone else vents about sex with their boyfriend, and we suddenly imagine them stripping and seducing us.

Of course, nobody wants to talk about experiencing these thoughts. They feel cumbersome, shameful, or flat-out wrong. But every therapist experiences them, and I believe this distraction is unavoidable. Distraction happens in everything we do: meditation, driving, grocery shopping, conversations with our best friends, and while giving and receiving therapy.

We are busy humans with fascinating internal systems, and we move through our days with complicated soundtracks dictating our thoughts and actions.

We spin through these distracting thoughts rapidly. They might come without any real warning or significance, but they disturb us nonetheless. Then we focus on how disturbed we feel. We shame ourselves for thinking about our pants or the economy or the looming pile of dishes in our kitchen sink back home. We beat on ourselves for doing a lousy job, for not being as present as our clients need us to be. At the same time, we also question if our client knows that we are distracted. Then we wonder what's wrong with us.

Talk about exhausting!

It's important to remember that therapists (shockingly) experience emotions and thoughts. Sometimes they relate to the countertransference we experience toward our clients; I discuss this in further detail in a later chapter. But other emotions and thoughts are far more shallow. A wailing ambulance passes by our office, and we wonder what happened. We remember that we're supposed to pay the water bill that day. We have to pee.

Distraction is inevitable. It's how we deal with it that matters.

Learn How to Move Back to the Present Moment

Distraction happens to every therapist, and we're not horrible people just because our minds drift aimlessly. But this doesn't mean we should spend our sessions contemplating whether to buy organic apples over regular ones. We do need to pay attention to our clients and attune to their needs. Here are some tips that can help you shift back into the present moment:

Accept the Thoughts Instead of Resisting Them

Many yogis insist that *savasana*, the last pose of the yoga practice, is the most challenging one. To the untrained eye, however, *savasana* looks like a nap. The pose entails lying flat on your back and breathing. There are no bends or twists or headstands that would impress your Instagram followers.

For years, I left yoga class just before the *savasana* pose because it seemed pointless. I sleep for about eight hours each night. Wasn't that enough rest and restoration? Besides, after ninety minutes of bending and sweating and comparing myself to the other yogis around me, I always needed to get home, call someone back, or do something I deemed incredibly important.

At that time, I also dismissed any benefits of mindfulness. To me, yoga wasn't about feeling present with my body or breath—it was an exercise designed to sculpt my ass and flatten my stomach. Mindfulness came after all those priorities, if it came at all.

I now recognize my naiveté. Mindfulness isn't about the complete absence of thoughts or feelings. That's an impossible feat. Mindfulness means accepting the present moment—it means surrendering and practicing self-compassion to move back into a conscious space.

We're allowed to be distracted. When we try to suppress those distractions, they become louder. In session, when a distracting thought arises, I recommend acknowledging it. Let that thought know you see it and you recognize it matters, but you're going to address it later. Try not to judge yourself for having the thought in the first place. Remember, we all experience distractions.

PS: In my yoga class, I now stay for the *savasana* pose. Every single time.

Pretend Someone Else Is Watching You

My graduate school required that we meet with clients at our university's mental health clinic. This clinic had two-way mirrors, and our classmates and professors observed our therapy sessions to give us feedback. This experience wasn't just anxiety-provoking, it was downright petrifying.

I'll say this: When people are watching me, I don't get bored. I don't have time to get bored. Yes, I become hyperaware, anxious, or insecure, but I certainly don't drift into idle thoughts about last night's dinner.

Now, years later, when my mind starts glazing over, I still pretend that I'm back in graduate school performing therapy in front of an audience. It works without fail.

Make It a Personal Mission to Move Away from Your Boredom

When we feel bored or restless with a client, these feelings typically indicate that we aren't working the session. We're not in the driver's seat, setting the tone and stage for our clients. Instead of asking thoughtful questions, we're letting things happen passively. We're bantering with meaningless small talk. We're allowing our client to ramble for three minutes about the controversial ending of their favorite TV show.

There are four pathways we can take to reignite our interest:

1. *Acknowledge Our Distraction to the Client*

When we admit our own shortcomings, we model being human to our clients. Sometimes, when my mind wanders, I acknowledge it as it's happening:

You know what? I got distracted for a minute right there. I'm very sorry. You matter so much to me, and I want to make sure I'm fully present for you. Can you repeat what you just said?

Clients don't expect us to remember every single word they tell us. But they expect to feel supported and understood. That means we need to treat them with kindness, respect, and professionalism. Acknowledging our fallibility helps us do just that.

2. *Pivot the Conversation*

Usually, we feel bored or distracted when the conversation feels meaningless. These feelings can emerge when we spend too long engaging in small talk. It can also happen when we repeat the same conversations we've had in the past.

At this point, it can be helpful to identify the pattern and suggest making a change. *Hey client, I realize we've spent a good amount of this session talking about your sister, and we can keep doing that if you need. But I want to revisit what we were discussing last week. What do you think?*

3. Address Our Emotions

I will discuss countertransference in more detail in future chapters. For now, I will note that all therapists have countertransference. Countertransference refers to transferring our emotions, thoughts, and biases onto clients. Depending on our own self-awareness, we may or may not be conscious of our countertransference.

I'm going to be honest with you. I'm finding it hard to stay focused right now. I think it's because we're jumping from topic to topic so quickly. It's making me feel a little distracted and even a bit anxious and restless. What about you?

4. Pretend You Are Your Client

I once worked with a timid woman who talked about the same issues every week without taking any real initiative to improve her circumstances. She was punctual and polite, and she presented as relatively cooperative. Yet I dreaded seeing her.

She had crippling self-esteem issues, most of which prevented her from making changes in her life. My patience began waning. I found myself frustrated with our pattern—frustrated with myself for not helping her, and frustrated with her for her own stagnation. We were both stuck.

One time, as she started talking, I suddenly imagined us switching places. For a moment, I sat in her body—a body older and seemingly more fragile than mine, a body that felt stiff and constricted. I felt her sandals on my feet and experienced the softness of the couch on my back. And then I felt her sadness and despair run through me.

This body experience wasn't intentional, and it felt strange. While sitting in my client's body, I could look at myself from her eyes. I could *feel* that my client needed me to slow down for her. She needed more patience—everyone tried to push her out of her comfort zone. At that moment, she needed my reassurance that she was good enough just the way she was.

I will not make the grandiose claim that we broke through our stagnation and made tremendous progress. Therapy doesn't work that way. Change takes time, and it can be painstakingly subtle.

I still struggled with this client. Throughout our work, I often had to remind myself to slow down and adjust my expectations. But I did learn how to bring myself into the present moment. And in doing so, I was able to give this woman more of my attention and support

Since working with that client, I've practiced this visualization technique countless times. It takes only a few seconds for it to work. Just take a moment and imagine being your client. Don't imagine what it must feel like. Imagine what it does feel like. As therapists, empathy is always our greatest asset. The more we tap in to it, the more present we are for our clients.

You Don't Need to Master Working with One Population Right Away (or Ever)

I worked in seven different training sites and had eight different supervisors during my years between graduate school and licensure. I recognize these are large numbers. My journey happened without any real plan.

But if I had the chance to do it again, I wouldn't change how I did it. My vast exposure to different styles of learning and clients has proven invaluable. Over the years, I have treated clients ranging from ages three to eighty-four. I've come across almost every disorder in the DSM, and I've worked with supervisors specializing in all types of theories. And while I often felt inadequate, I always recognized that I was learning and growing.

Many therapists think they need to know their niche or population right after completing school. I don't think this is necessary. Often, we don't know if we like working with a specific population until we start working with them. Similarly, it's not uncommon for therapists to discover they really don't want to work with that group of people!

I recommend keeping an open mind during your training years. Get exposure. Learn new ways of doing things. Many therapists stumble into a population or theory without seeking it out. Stay curious about what you don't know.

Learn to Accept Unconventional and Nonlinear Progress

Therapy remains beautifully and stubbornly flawed because humans are beautifully and stubbornly flawed. If we choose the easy way and start pigeonholing progress, we risk missing what our work truly represents.

Our clients' problems sit on top of other problems, and we can lose ourselves in untangling the stories that define the lives of the people we treat. To add more complications, professionals constantly argue about the best ways to understand or intervene with treatment. But before we even attempt to measure progress, we must identify the obstacles that make measurements challenging. Here are some considerations:

Obstacle #1: Clients Lie (Both Intentionally and Unintentionally)

Often during the course of therapy patients may describe examples of deception in their life—some incident when they have either concealed or distorted information about themselves. Using here-and-now rabbit ears, I find such an admission an excellent opportunity to inquire about what lies they have told me during the course of therapy. There is always some concealment, some information withheld because of shame, because of some particular way they wish me to regard them. —Irvin Yalom, The Gift of Therapy

I know I've lied to every therapist I've ever had. I also believe that most, if not all, of my clients have lied to me.

We often label lying as a disloyal, malicious, and manipulative act. We categorize it as something that must be fixed. But most lying happens so automatically. It's a primitive defense mechanism protecting us from the bottomless abyss of shame. And it's also not always intentional or even easy to define.

I imagine many clients enter their first therapy session like they enter a first date. Before a first date, we obsess about what to wear and what to say. During dinner, we attempt to dazzle our date with witty jokes and fascinating stories about volunteering abroad and saving the sea turtles. We slow down—we might eat a quarter of our meal and savor our wine slowly. In both our actions and words, we highlight our strengths while downplaying or omitting our insecurities.

Many clients enter therapy in a similar fashion. They're cautious. They may rehearse what they plan to say ahead of time. They might minimize their symptoms. They study our bookshelves and certificates and the pillows on our couch—they take whatever information they can get to assess whether we're the right fit.

But what happens when our first date goes well? When that stranger graduates into a partner or spouse? We naturally become more comfortable. We start arriving at the restaurant without thinking so much about our appearance or what we want to say. Instead of long, mesmerizing conversations about love and life, we might spend dinner bitching about our boss or our coworker's new car. We text and check our email and interrupt each other. Were we lying on that first date? Or can truth exist in different layers?

Think about how therapy unfolds itself. The poised client has a meltdown about her fears of unlovability. The client who denied trauma reveals that her parents beat her. The sober client shares that he relapsed months ago. Were these clients blatantly lying to us? Sometimes, yes. But can we acknowledge that we all have varying shades of truth? And can we recognize that our fears of how others perceive us influence everything we do?

Think about all the times you lie in a day. If your coworker asks for your opinion about her new sweater, do you admit that it looks horrific? When you're having lunch with your family, do you tell your mother-in-law that her chicken tastes like garlicky rubber? If a new date asks what you did last weekend, how likely are you to divulge that you spent fourteen hours lying naked on the couch with a jar of Nutella watching Netflix?

Our clients lie to us for many reasons. First, they want us to like them. Many clients fantasize about being our favorite client. They present well because they want us to feel proud and impressed by them. Often, they've had countless experiences related to feeling like they've let other people down. Their efforts to please emerge from the transference they experience toward us; I explore this more deeply in a later chapter.

Sometimes, clients lie because they know our positions of authority and power, particularly when it comes to mandated reporting. They avoid disclosing sensitive material related to issues like suicidal thoughts or child abuse. They worry the truth will get them into trouble. At times, they are completely correct.

Clients also lie because they want to test us. Sometimes, they want to determine what we remember and what we forget. Are we really a safe person? Are we truly trustworthy? Can we actually hold the pain we promise we can hold? Most lies come from a place of hopeful truth.

Finally, if you still don't think your clients lie to you, you are deluding yourself. To lie is to be human. It's not always about decoding the lies—it's about remembering that the very best lies often sound like the very best truths.

Obstacle #2: Trust Can Take a Very, Very Long Time

Therapists often act like building rapport with a client is a box we check on a standard treatment plan. Without rapport, we don't have a safe therapeutic relationship. And without a safe therapeutic relationship, our clients will struggle to let us help them.

That said, we must also remember that trust takes time. And we can't always quantify the time. It doesn't "just happen" in sessions three or six or twenty-four. We can't plan when trust happens, and it doesn't happen all at once. Trust is sensitive and fragile—it can take so long to build, and just a single comment or expression can destroy it.

Clients logically know that therapists should be compassionate and nonjudgmental. But knowing is different from feeling, and so many clients come to us with severe histories of betrayal. They have trusted the wrong people, and they have been deeply wounded. They have been shamed and rejected for sharing their truths. To cope with this incredible pain, they have learned to guard and conceal themselves. Even if they want to let their guard down, that desire alone doesn't make the task easier.

We must remember that nobody inherently owes us their trust. However, I know some therapists find this concept confusing. After all, why would our clients sacrifice their time and money if they didn't trust us? Doesn't that make therapy pointless? Doesn't that defeat the purpose of getting help?

Clients want to trust us—they want to trust us desperately. We all long for connection; everyone wants to feel safe and secure with another person. Although our clients desire these benefits, they also arrive to therapy with defenses and fears. Some come to us with extensive histories of breached trust or rejection. Again, many of our clients initiate therapy because they know therapy is designed to be supportive. However, knowing is different from feeling. We can't just turn on trust like it's a light switch. We have to foster it in every interaction we have with our clients.

Obstacle #3: Progress in One Area Can Reveal Flaws Somewhere Else

I once received a referral for a client recently discharged from a hospital after a suicide attempt. She came to me with a long rap sheet of various psychiatric diagnoses, ranging from borderline personality disorder to schizophrenia to multiple substance use disorders. She also had a history of severe childhood trauma as well as several restraining orders against violent ex-partners.

In therapy, she presented as insightful and eager for therapy. She listened to my suggestions about possible coping skills, and she integrated some of them immediately. Every week, she beamed with pride as she reported her successes. She began meditating. She took walks when she felt overwhelmed. She even journaled about her feelings a few nights a week. Best of all, she no longer felt suicidal. She believed she had been given a second chance in life. I was so proud of her, and I was so proud of myself. We were doing it!

A few months later, she told me that she had begun dating her coworker. She described him as different from the others—he was sensitive and caring, and he had his own complex history of psychiatric illness and childhood trauma. She shared how much they had in common, how much she felt they understood each other. A few weeks later, she arrived at her session with a bruise on her face. When I asked about it, she claimed that she tripped on the curb and fell.

The next week, I saw another bruise on her arm.

If we froze our treatment right there, would I be able to indicate if I had made progress with my client? She was no longer suicidal, and she didn't attempt suicide again in the many more months we continued working together. But our alliance was invariably stacked against a serious risk factor, one that could have led her back to the same dark place.

Improvements in one concentrated area can have the effect of improvement in other areas. A client is no longer suicidal, and their self-esteem improves. A client moves to a new neighborhood, and they make new friends. However, clients often jump from one issue to the next. They cycle through traumas and crises. They take five steps forward in one part of their lives, but they tumble down the staircase somewhere else.

For new therapists, this reality may feel discouraging, and that's because it can be. After all, many clients come to us desperately wanting a change in their lives. And we want to hand them their progress in a neatly wrapped package with a distinct before-and-after timeline. We want to give them the solutions that will heal them from their longstanding distress.

But progress doesn't work that way because life doesn't work that way.

Obstacle #4: The Client's Goal Isn't Always the Best Goal

I worked with a middle-aged man who wanted help for his depression. In our intake session, he complained of feeling more sad and tired than usual.

He reported feeling apathetic at work, bored with his friends, and confused over whether he still loved his wife.

By our sixth session, I agreed that he was, in fact, very depressed. It remained unclear if he loved his wife. He did, however, love his opioid prescription. The previous year, after an intensive back surgery, he discovered how much physical and emotional relief the pills offered.

He didn't want to quit. Since his doctor prescribed them, my client didn't identify his use as problematic. Yet, he took his medication far more frequently, and he had bought more pills from a coworker and online. He had overdosed once, but he insisted that happened because he hadn't eaten much the day before. In our sessions, he continued to emphasize that he just needed to focus on his depression and his marriage. He didn't want to lose his wife or children. If anything, he told me, the painkillers helped him feel less depressed.

Therapists working with acute, high-risk populations (substance use disorders, eating disorders, complex trauma, psychotic disorders) see this discrepancy all the time. They know about denial and minimization and intellectualization.

Unfortunately, my client's opioid use became more of an issue as our treatment evolved. He refused to acknowledge it as a problem. Eventually, he stopped coming to therapy, and I don't know what happened to him.

As therapists, it's important that we recognize the hierarchy of treatment needs. Identifying and treating certain issues must precede others. However, a mismatch in priorities can certainly impact progress, and it can also create issues within the therapeutic relationship itself. After all, we aren't supposed to have an agenda. We are, however, supposed to keep our clients safe. At times, these issues can and will intersect.

Obstacle #5: We Rarely Receive Productive Feedback

Aside from the occasional transcription video, nobody sees us in the therapy room. Our colleagues, supervisors, or spouses can't watch us perform.

Although we discuss cases, we don't receive accurate feedback about our skills, because nobody truly knows what we're saying or doing. This lack of feedback makes measuring progress difficult. We may believe we're doing a good job, but it's challenging to recognize our blind spots if we ourselves are blind to them! Likewise, even if we know something isn't working, we may not know what that something is.

Additionally, most clients won't provide us with direct feedback. We aren't Amazon purchases. Clients don't rush online to post their glowing or scathing reviews about our services. We're not even allowed to solicit testimonials. This dynamic leaves us in a vulnerable position. We rely on clients to be honest about their feelings toward us. At the same time, we must straddle the reality of knowing that most clients avoid confrontation, want to please us, and blame themselves if and when things go wrong in therapy.

Obstacle #6: Things Get Worse Before They Get Better

During my training, I worked with a young woman who wanted to improve her confidence. When we first began meeting, she was in a chaotic relationship with her boyfriend, and they had just moved in together. She had a long history of tumultuous relationships, all of which she described as having ended destructively.

Together, we explored the roots of her interpersonal problems. She had extremely low self-esteem, and she depended on men to validate her. She found stable partners boring and unappealing, and she frequently cheated in her relationships. But it took several months for her to tell me that her father had molested her when she was a little girl.

After that revelation, she didn't show up to the next session. Or the one after that. Three weeks later, when she did arrive, she confessed that she believed I had tricked her into sharing her trauma history. She then declared that she never wanted to talk about her past to me again.

Our professors and the master therapists warn us that things can get worse before they get better, and we hear this cliché all the time. But many therapists struggle to understand that this phase can last for a supremely long time. I'm not talking about riding it out for a few sessions. I'm talking about months and even possibly years.

My client felt gutted by having revealed her molestation, and our therapy continued to be rough for several months. Every time I met with her, I felt guilty. Wasn't talking it out supposed to be helpful? Didn't we need to work through this trauma? And when was she going to start feeling better?

Therapists struggle when they watch their clients struggle. First, we care about their well-being. Additionally, we often assume that a happy client indicates that we are doing our job successfully. But we can't just measure progress by a client's level of happiness. In fact, happiness isn't always measurable or achievable. Sometimes, we must measure progress based on other factors like increased self-awareness or strengthening boundaries or changing negative behaviors.

We must remember that our clients may remain in the "getting worse" phase even after they leave treatment. This phenomenon is common when we don't control the termination, which I discuss in a later chapter.

Remember That Books Don't Always Tell the Truth

I have a love-hate relationship with many psychotherapy books. Why? Because even when therapists try to educate their readers and showcase their weaknesses, they inevitably brag about their brilliance.

As a professional content and copywriter, I'll let you in on an insider secret. All successful writing needs to be engaging, compelling, and crafted to appeal to a target demographic. In other words, good writers can be manipulative. When we write to an audience, we do so with the reader in mind.

Successful writers often research the hell out of their prospective readers. Regardless of the industry, they understand the competition, and they aim to make their writing the best.

These intentions aren't malicious. Nobody wants to harm or trick their readers. But talented writing is an art. We can organize even the most banal information in a way that creates intriguing stories. We know how to provoke and how to engage. We know what to highlight and what to avoid.

Moreover, writers work with qualified professionals who refine their thoughts even more. Many eyes look over a manuscript before it ever reaches the masses. Professional editors sharpen the story; graphic designers create beautiful, eye-catching covers; and marketers run campaigns and sponsored advertisements to drive sales. Successful writing is a business—even for therapists.

And even as I write this book, I am intending to sell it. This isn't a secret, and it shouldn't be. I love writing, and I love helping people, but the prospect of earning money motivates me to do work I wouldn't ordinarily do for free. Compensation doesn't make my information less important. If anything, the financial gain makes my information more relevant. I want the finished product to be worth the reader's monetary investment.

As I mentioned, we never truly know what happens in a therapy session. It's easy for therapists who write about their work to embellish a vignette; beautify an exchange of dialogue; and smooth out long, awkward silences. Talented writers may know how to write about therapy more than they know how to conduct therapy.

This process reminds me how I feel when I watch reality television. I can't move past my awareness that the plot and characters are contrived and staged. I always consider what the producers aren't showing me. I know they control and contort the information they choose to share with their audience. They create a story to tell a story—writers are not so different.

Therapists love to share ideas. But, in addition to help people, it's reasonable for us to like money, exposure, and the possibility of exciting opportunities. Publishing a successful book is one way to start walking down that lucrative path. I wrote this book because I wanted to offer reassurance and optimism for struggling therapists. But I'd be lying if I said I didn't want all the other benefits!

I will keep reading psychotherapy books, and I hope you do, too. The ideas aren't wrong. The concepts themselves can be inspirational, brilliant, and essential to our work. Just be mindful that even master therapists aren't perfect all the time. A good writer isn't always a good therapist.

Understand That You'll Never Be the Right Age

I was twenty-one years old when I started graduate school, the youngest student in my cohort. My small frame, baby face, and lack of real-world experience only exaggerated my obvious youth. Shortly after graduation, I began working in a junior high school. During my first week, a teacher yelled at me to hurry to class after the bell rang. I couldn't fault her. Without makeup and heels, I still passed for a teenager.

For years, I watched as new clients sized me up and down. Even if they didn't ask outright, the question was always the same: *For fuck's sake, how old are you?*

One of my closest colleagues became a therapist in her early fifties. She had spent twenty years working in an unrelated industry. Her age created similar challenges. Surrounded by peers the same age as her children, she felt hyper-conscious in graduate school. Where I thought I was too young to relate to my clients, she believed she was too old. Where I thought they might consider me too immature and unrefined, she worried they would find her too outdated and out-of-touch.

We will never be the "perfect age" to be therapists. No matter our ages, some clients will benefit from it, and others will have a problem with it.

We invariably hold biases about age, but we hold biases about everything. Our clients make automatic assumptions based on every detail we provide them.

And since we don't offer our clients much, they base their judgments on whatever is accessible: our hair, our car, our clothes, the wrinkles we have or don't have, the food wrappers on our desks. These assumptions create an influential narrative. Regardless of the accuracy, the assumptions connect dots and illustrate a picture of who we are. Clients don't want us to be blank templates. They want to know we're human, and they will latch on to any shred of human evidence they can find from us.

My best advice is to lean into this narrative. Your age is yours. While it doesn't define you, it is a fixed part of you. Our job isn't necessarily to challenge the client's biases. Our job is to be authentic, and our authenticity might sometimes fit into their biases. Other times, it won't. Both scenarios are okay.

Don't Forget That You're Going to Die

In my final editing stages, I considered deleting this part after my friend commented, *I'm sorry, but I can't figure out why this section is here.* I have decided to keep it because I think the following information is integral to our well-being.

I want to remind everyone that I'm going to die, and you're going to die, and it's guaranteed to happen. Thankfully, I don't know when or how my time on this planet will end.

Remember the essence of your mortality. Tuck it into your pocket and stroke your finger on it every so often. There is nothing like the thought of death that makes us want to cherish life.

If you struggle to remember your mortality, I recommend you imagine yourself on your deathbed. I know this sounds morbid, but life is morbid, and we spend so much of our time obsessing over trivial mental clutter. In this deathbed exercise, scan through all the past and current events, people, and places in your life. Don't spend too long in the space—only a minute or so. Then visualize yourself drifting into death, settling into the depths of the darkest night.

What did you feel right there? Anxiety, probably. But what did you feel anxious about? The regrets you carry with you? The worry that you've wasted time? The missed moments or lack of taking risks? This mortality exercise isn't about discrediting our careers. It's about reminding ourselves that life is incredibly short and precious. We don't need to have "perfect therapist" etched on our headstones.

We are going to die, and life is so much more than the sum of our careers.

We're all going to die. But before we do that, we need to learn how to live.

CHAPTER 3:

HOW TO GET IN THE RIGHT THERAPIST MINDSET

Acting like a therapist happens long before you ever sit with your first client. Having the right mindset is key for your success. In this chapter, I discuss everything I wish I knew before I started.

Know the Limits of Graduate School

At fifteen years old, before I learned how to drive a car, I received my provisional permit. In California, you receive this permit after passing a driver's knowledge test. The test proves our comprehension and renders us fit to sit behind the wheel. But knowing every law and every trick doesn't mean much until you actually drive.

Graduate school teaches the foundational principles of psychotherapy. We learn the laws and ethics, and we receive bite-size samples of theory, interventions, and psychoeducation. But until we do therapy, we really have no way of knowing what therapy feels like. School teaches us the logic of the work, but only experience teaches us the emotion of it.

If you are a prospective or current student, my warning may sound discouraging. After all, school is expensive, time-consuming, and mentally exhausting. We want it to be a worthy sacrifice. Remember that we rarely feel prepared for the first time we do anything. Have you ever tried a new hobby? Do you remember the first time? Maybe you bought the gear and watched the tutorials, but actually *doing it* probably felt so awkward. You needed lots of practice before you started gaining any real semblance of confidence. It's the same with becoming a therapist.

Understand Your Relationships Can, Will, and Should Evolve

I ended a serious and long-term relationship during my first month of graduate school. We dated throughout college, and we were at the pivotal point of musing over wedding dates and potential baby names. Our relationship was entirely dysfunctional. We were young and brimming with hot emotion; we were dramatic and reactive, but I believed all these problems could improve in time.

In becoming therapists, we learn about the nitty-gritty patterns of human behavior. Simultaneously, by understanding these patterns, we engage in a deep and rigorous self-analysis. We have no choice but to also look inward, to examine how we operate in the world. And while this soul-searching offers tantalizing insight, all self-awareness has the potential to be painful.

I fundamentally changed while in graduate school, but I know that change was necessary. The end of the toxic relationship with my boyfriend forced me to focus on myself. I needed to work on my self-esteem and learn how to set boundaries with other people. My priorities shifted, and I lost some friends as a result. There was immense grief associated with these changes; I often felt lonely and skeptical about my choices.

In graduate school, I started prioritizing my self-care and emotional well-being. I spent many hours flopped on therapy couches exploring my fears and insecurities. I began meditating. I journaled about my feelings. I spent a lot of time on hiking trails and yoga mats. I wrote down my gratitude every single night.

When I met my husband, I felt ready to embrace his love. I knew I deserved a healthy, compassionate partner. However, if I hadn't worked on myself, I might have sabotaged the relationship altogether. I might have acted in the same, childish ways I acted with previous partners. Instead, I was able to give and accept love.

Over the years, some of my relationships have changed or dissolved entirely. I won't pretend those losses aren't painful or frustrating or scary. Choosing to embrace your emotional well-being does have a cost. However, if you value emotional wellness and personal growth, the pain is a necessary part of the process.

Cultivate a Connection with a Professor or Supervisor

When I was in college, I worked part-time as a tutor for high school students. Most of my students sat across from me, bored and disengaged, trying to finish their assignments as quickly as possible. I understood their apathy. Who wants to hang out with their tutor?

But some of my students showed curiosity. They asked thoughtful questions and demonstrated critical-thinking skills. Some students demonstrated a keen interest in my life. They initiated polite conversation about my weekend, my college classes, the contents of my sandwich.

I loved these curious students. Their intelligence or test scores didn't matter to me. What mattered was that they made *me* feel more fulfilled and validated. They made me feel like my job meant something.

Professors who teach psychotherapy want to pass their knowledge and expertise on to the next generation of therapists. They want rooms full of people with passion and curiosity. They want students to ask questions. Nothing feels more daunting than standing before a group of thirty bored students.

Professors and supervisors also hold power. When I say power, I mean that they can dramatically affect your success in terms of internships, scholarships, or long-term career options. We all benefit from having someone who can vouch for us. Ideally, this person will:

- write an excellent letter of recommendation if needed.

- act as a reference when applying for internships or jobs.

- provide appropriate and helpful guidance.

If you're a new therapist, start thinking about this goal immediately. Make yourself memorable. Ask questions. Attend office hours. Ask them about the contents of their sandwich. Be active and engaged in conversation, and show up ready to work and learn.

Master Time Management

I've worked since I was fifteen, and I juggled three jobs during my first semester of graduate school. I felt determined to prepare myself financially for my future, but my jam-packed schedule was downright grueling. I don't recommend my strategy to anyone.

When school started, a few of my professors expressed that they wanted us to devote our full attention to our studies. They didn't want us working. Unfortunately, their aspirations weren't practical for many students. Some of us needed to work. We needed health insurance and a stable income to pay mortgages or support our families.

Regardless of your circumstances, all therapists benefit from auditing their time-management skills. In what areas do you tend to waste time? We all do it, but most of us aren't even aware of our biggest offenders. Do you scroll mindlessly through social media? Do you laze in front of the television? Do you say yes to every obligation, which ultimately leads you to feel completely rushed?

Today, I consider myself reasonably successful with time management. Maybe it's because I've always balanced multiple obligations, but I know it's also because I have massive control and perfectionism tendencies. Either way, I'm highlighting some of my favorite tips:

Audit How You Spend Every Working Hour for One Week

After having my son, I took time away from being a therapist and focused more on my writing career. By that point, I had been freelancing for years, but I knew I needed to optimize how I managed my time. I downloaded a time-tracker application to see how long it took me to complete specific projects—I figured having this awareness could help me best set my freelance rates.

The exercise of time tracking yielded many surprises. Where I thought I spent about ten minutes a day emailing prospective leads, it added up to hours throughout the week. Where I thought a certain assignment took me an hour, it actually took two. I also wasted *so much time.* Emails, Facebook, coffee breaks, making silly memes—but once I learned where that time went, I could cinch in my hours to work more productively.

I committed to a month of this auditing process. It was arduous, but I became more efficient with working each week. It almost became a competition with myself. I still track my time when I freelance, and the information is invaluable. Knowing where my time goes allows me to quote client deadlines properly, set appropriate fees, and outsource various tasks. To this day, my tracking is absolutely one of the best choices I've ever made in my business.

Make Red, Yellow, Green To-Do Lists

When I work, I make red, yellow, and green lists before I start any particular task. The reds are the most imminent and nonnegotiable tasks. They have to get done, so I prioritize them first. Yellows are important, but they are less time-sensitive and critical than the reds. I move to yellows only after I complete the red tasks. I reserve greens for last. Some days, I get to them. Most days, I don't.

Ban Distractions

I'm a diehard multitasker, and my flexibility has served me well throughout life. But this strategy can also be incredibly stressful and taxing. I bounce from task to task, and I know this constant bouncing results in wasted productivity.

We crave distraction. Although most of us complain about our procrastination habits, we forget that procrastination is also fun. Who wants to do homework when we can watch movies? Why study when we can go out with friends?

The best way for me to ban distractions is by prohibiting them during my red tasks. It's a cold-turkey approach, but I find it works for me. I also build in ten-minute breaks every thirty minutes. I realize spending one-third of my working time taking breaks sounds excessive, but this permits me to work in longer chunks without completely draining my energy.

Remember That Motivation Is Optional, But Discipline Is Necessary

Motivation is fickle because it's a feeling. Feelings, as we know, are fleeting. It isn't a surprise that most people struggle to follow through with their New Year's resolutions, weight-loss goals, or budgets. It's because we usually abandon new habits once they start becoming challenging. The burger tastes better than the salad. Buying a pretty new purse feels more exciting than investing in a retirement plan.

Discipline, on the other hand, is an action. We can discipline ourselves regardless of our feelings. I discipline myself to brush my teeth, and I brush my teeth whether I'm happy, sad, or scared. Do I always want to do this task? No, of course not. Sometimes I'm exhausted and I just want to go to sleep. But I don't question whether I should brush my teeth because I'm disciplined to do it.

Many people who struggle with discipline also struggle with poor time management. That's because they wait to feel motivated to discipline themselves. Stop waiting. Start doing. It's just like brushing your teeth.

Take Care Of Your Finances

It's no secret that many therapists complete school with exorbitant amounts of student loan debt. Lenders chase after your money soon after graduation, and they will hunt you down with a vengeance. At the same time, many therapists accept stressful positions for atrocious pay. Some of us must work multiple jobs or pursue side hustles to stay afloat.

Financial insecurity impacts our personal lives. But it also creates an insidious ripple effect in our professional endeavors. To highlight my point, I'd like to share a few common examples of how financial stress can show up in our professional choices:

- Accepting a cash-pay client even if the issues are out of the therapist's scope of competence.

- Avoiding terminating with a client when it's ethically appropriate to do so.

- Working for an unethical organization due to the stable paycheck and benefits.

- Dramatically exaggerating symptoms to meet criteria for a diagnosis reimbursable by insurance companies.

As to the issue of how you spend your money—this isn't a personal finance book, and I'm not here to lecture anyone about their spending habits. However, I encourage you to reflect on your relationship with money. We already work in a field saturated with low pay scales, and many therapists find themselves in defeating cycles of feeling overworked and underpaid. They live paycheck to paycheck, and they're in a perpetual state of either fear or denial about a minor emergency decimating their savings.

Your financial health is part of your well-being, and today's stressors can become tomorrow's emergencies. If you're neglecting this part of your life, take the time to identify small changes you can make today. Maybe it's tracking your spending and reducing discretionary purchases. Maybe it's setting a timeline for paying down your debts. Perhaps it's negotiating for a higher salary. We live in a world dictated by access to or lack of access to money. While the rules may not feel fair, we must accept this reality.

CHAPTER 4:

HOW TO ACTUALLY PREPARE FOR YOUR FIRST THERAPY SESSION

The truth is that being a therapist changes all of your relationships and many friends and family will get left behind. You will face your own terrifying demons every week, and this takes its toll. You will be underpaid and underappreciated. You will see people when they are at their worst and you will be expected to present yourself at your best. Every time.
—Jeffrey Kottler, On Being a Therapist

You framed your diploma. You bought the professional clothes. If you have your own office (lucky you!), you devote an entire weekend afternoon brainstorming your decorations.

Succulents or orchids? I can't keep an orchid alive, but I'm not sure if I can keep succulents alive, either. How much sunlight is streaming into my office? How much sunlight do plants need again? Maybe I should just get some fake plants. Are noise machines necessary? Is this throw pillow too flashy? No, the rest of the office is too color-coordinated, and this pillow will show that I'm eccentric. And what about a rug? Do I need one? Does anybody NEED a rug? Yikes! Do I even have money for this? How many clocks do I need again?

Congrats! You're a therapist! Now what?

Focus on Being a Growth-Oriented Therapist

When we were in high school, my best friend enrolled in cosmetology school. Like therapists, all student cosmetologists must complete a designated number of training hours to obtain licensure. They accrue these hours by practicing their hair, skin, and nail services on paying customers.

For years, I went to my friend's school for my own haircuts. The services were heavily discounted; a cut and color cost me less than half of the rate than that of a traditional salon. Moreover, the customer service and professionalism impressed me. At these schools, instructors patrolled the floors to monitor their students. They often assisted with techniques and touch-ups. At the end of the service, the instructor would approve its completion. This supervision benefited everyone. It helped the stylists improve their skills and confidence, and it ensured my approval as a client.

The student stylists never hid the fact that they were learning. They didn't pretend to be experts, and they didn't believe they were above asking for help. I respect this process tremendously.

I'd love for training therapists to take on this same mentality. I'd like them to recognize they're learning, and that they don't need to know everything. They need to work hard, but they're allowed to have limitations. The goal isn't having all the experience or knowledge. The goal is to have ongoing movement toward growth. This is a value that can and should continue throughout one's professional career. Here is a comparison between the mindsets of what

I call "growth-oriented therapists" and "stagnant therapists."

Growth-Oriented Therapists	Stagnant Therapists
Ask difficult questions to clients (even if they feel uncomfortable and provocative).	Maintain surface-level conversation and often play it safe in dialogue with clients.
Present mistakes, weaknesses, and concerns to their supervisor, with the intention to learn from them. They are active in supervision, and they offer practical suggestions and feedback to their colleagues.	Sugarcoat or downplay issues in sessions. They tend to focus only on what is going well. They share minimally in supervision, as they don't want to be judged by their supervisor or colleagues.
Focus on client growth instead of client approval. They address pain and confront clients when appropriate.	Struggle to accept hardships within the therapeutic relationship. They often hold back in confronting clients.
Walk into the session with a sense of purpose and the mindset of practicing their skills. They feel a sense of control over the session.	Walk into the session feeling scattered. They're at the mercy of whatever the client brings that day, and they often lose focus.

Use conceptualization skills to interpret the client's overall presentation. They consider what is being said, but they also consider what might be omitted.	Lack conceptualization skills. They take client content and disclosures at face value, and they become distracted or overwhelmed by content details presented in session.
Understand the overall fluidity of therapy. They recognize that growth occurs mostly outside of sessions and that therapy is the catalyst for change (and not the change itself).	View sessions as separate entities. They judge sessions as "good" or "bad" based on variables like if a client made a significant breakthrough or responded well to a particular intervention
Have insight into internal strengths and weaknesses. They feel motivated to work on weaknesses and readily accept feedback in doing so.	May have insight into internal strengths and weaknesses. But, they feel paralyzed or doomed by their weaknesses and may become defensive over them.
Understand that therapy often has unknown outcomes. They conceptualize how clients might react, but they aren't tethered to this expectation.	Want controllable outcomes. They either avoid conceptualization altogether or they expect themselves to know exactly what to do.

During my book revision stages, a reader pointed out that cosmetologists have very different roles from therapists. She expressed that a therapist making a poor judgment call could be far more detrimental than a stylist giving someone a bad haircut. She had a valid point, and I debated changing my cosmetology reference. Ultimately, I kept it. Why? Because the career doesn't matter. Every profession has some form of apprenticeship. Cosmetologists, therapists, doctors, lawyers, plumbers—everyone learns by practicing, and everyone feels embarrassed when they make a mistake. My best friend, the cosmetologist, once called me in tears after she butchered a client's hair. The client left the salon feeling furious. Who am I to claim my best friend's pain was less important than mine?

I want to remind you that your training status isn't a secret. If you're a trainee, intern, or associate, you have already disclosed your status to clients. You're under supervision, and you work under someone else's license. Subsequently, nobody expects you to be an expert. But too many therapists fear making mistakes.

I understand it's challenging to discern which risks are appropriate to take. Nobody wants to cause irreversible harm to their clients. But that's why we have supervision and training. That's why we work under someone else. This is your time to experiment and grow—you'll never have such ample opportunity again.

Remember, Your Career Is More Than a Calling

Are you a therapist because it's your calling? A calling sounds so special, doesn't it? It's like the world must thank you for your undeniable selflessness.

And yet, I argue that we must restructure and even dismantle this concerning stereotype. Aren't we frustrated with people telling us we can't ask for money because our work represents a sacrificial labor of love? Aren't we tired of proving to the medical community that psychotherapy is an evidence-based profession?

Callings are nice, but they aren't enough.

I'm not suggesting it's wrong to want to be a therapist. Let it be a calling. So many people feel unhappy in their jobs—if being a therapist makes you feel fulfilled, consider yourself lucky. But our work cannot just be a sum of being called to do it. We earn professional degrees, and we adhere to strict laws and ethics and evidence-based treatment. Our predecessors created and implemented fantastic theories based on dedicated time and effort.

I believe the term *calling* cheapens the professional aspect of our career. If people assume that being a therapist inherently brings complete fulfillment, they may disregard other parts of the job—they may overlook the need for decent living wages, professional boundaries, and a reasonable work-life balance.

Callings can also sound demeaning—it's like we are meant to do therapy without any real applied effort. This isn't true. Some therapists are inherently talented, but all successful therapists need education, skills, and practice. We must remember we are healthcare professionals and trained experts in treating mental illness. We spend significant money and time to cultivate our craft. At times, we save lives. Our work matters. Let's rise to that.

Accept All the Anxieties

A client once called me a fucking idiot to my face. I had unintentionally offended her, and she responded by hurling that insult. The memory is humorous now, but it wasn't then. Her words stung, but not because they insulted me. They stung because her words echoed my deepest fears. I already thought I was failing. I already felt incapable and incompetent to help the clients sitting across from me.

If you work in this field long enough, you'll also be insulted, cursed at, and rejected by your clients. If it never happens to you, you're either perfect, or you're not taking enough risks. Every therapist will experience some variation of feeling like a fucking idiot.

Being a therapist is scary. The anxiety doesn't necessarily disappear, but we learn to adapt it. With time and experience, we gain confidence in ourselves and in our skills. Although the anxiety often feels paralyzing at first, you must trust that it eventually subsides.

People constantly ask me how they can feel less anxious when starting work as a therapist. I don't have any useful advice beyond accepting the fear. I found comfort knowing everyone else felt equally terrified.

If you aren't scared, you're either narcissistic or you don't care about doing good work. Neither of these scenarios is ideal for a beginning therapist.

All therapists experience anxiety. Please read that again until it sinks in. We're wired to feel scared in new situations. We don't want to fail and disappoint others or ourselves. But fear isn't an excuse to back down. You don't need to run from it. If you run, you'll be running in the wrong direction. Similarly, you don't need to overcome and conquer it, either. You just need to make room for it. You must act regardless of the emotion.

Therapists sit with raw emotion for a living. We dissect and play with vulnerability, and then we often go home and reflect on everything we said or wished we'd said. The work is messy, and we inevitably doubt, discredit, and shame ourselves.

But we are not failures, even if we think we are. Accept that those negative thoughts will arise. Accept that they don't indicate your truth. Cry. Eat chocolate. Journal. Bitch it out to your own therapist. You will recover from this moment.

As therapists, we help people move through their fears in almost every session. It only makes sense that we learn this skill ourselves.

Practice Letting Go of Controlling the Room

The therapeutic dance is as strange as it is alluring. Our clients expose their vulnerable selves, and we sit in our chairs encouraging their vulnerability. We anticipate their full disclosure, while we cautiously scrutinize our own revelations. We anticipate their discomfort—it shapes our sessions. We cheer it on and hold it, promising we'll never pass judgment. We feel honored that we see the sides of our clients that they hide from their best friends and spouses. At times, we become intoxicated with the power and adoration they seem to have for us.

It is no secret that many therapists have control issues. We want results, and we want them on our terms. In the room, we bring our baggage to sessions—our low self-esteem and self-doubt, our fear of rejection, our desire to please others. Sometimes we understand and recognize this baggage, but sometimes we don't.

Consequently, when things don't go according to plan, we might panic. We might blame ourselves or our client or the process of therapy. We might question if what we're doing even matters. Although we love when our clients can be vulnerable, we might feel tricked and connived when the vulnerability monster comes knocking on our own door.

And the more we attempt to hold on to control, the more out of control we feel. And when we feel out of control, we react. We punish our clients with general assumptions (*They can't be helped, and I'm not going to even try.*). We skip over listening and try to fix with direct advice or solutions. We hone in on issues that don't matter, and we waste time in session talking about the weather or yesterday's lunch. Instead of reflecting on the relationship, we blame ourselves or our clients when things don't progress. Then we try to reel ourselves back into a semblance of control. We think about which intervention we need to do next. We return to linear treatment goals with specified dates and objectives.

In almost every facet of life, control is a complete illusion. We never have it, even when we play it really safe, and our clients cooperate with our expectations. As therapists, we can only control ourselves in the therapy room. If we are working with one individual, we have 50 percent of the control. If we are working with more than one person, we have less than that.

Letting go of controlling the room requires a lifetime of work in learning acceptance. We all struggle with expectations for our clients. We all want certain things to manifest. While it feels gratifying to watch a client evolve and transform, we don't own their timelines. We may be experts in compassion and emotional guidance, but we are not deities who determine human behavior.

Only when we fully surrender our expectations of our client, the session, and the moment itself, can we become truly present.

Don't Lose Yourself in the Details

We often distract ourselves with trivial information presented to us in session. We might ask clarifying questions to encourage our clients to share potentially irrelevant story details. Usually, our intentions are good. We want to build rapport and connect with our clients. We want to demonstrate that we care about their lives and that we are listening.

But our efforts can become misguided. Typically, we only have one hour (if that) to meet with our clients each week. We should not spend this hour asking them to only recount events or get us up to speed with their week. Our clients meet with us because they need help unpacking those experiences. If we don't help them unpack, they leave our office without insight or solutions. They might feel heard, but they won't feel motivated to work on their issues.

To avoid getting lost in the details of a client's content, we must think less about singular experiences and more about persistent patterns. The patterns can be behavioral, emotional, cognitive, relational—they can be anything. The theories you have learned will help you identify these patterns more readily; I will discuss this concept in a later chapter. But for now, it's important to remember to move away from thinking about a client's stories as single entities. Instead, try to consider how each experience represents a fundamental link in a chain.

Let's say your client comes to you complaining about his psychiatrist. He insists that the psychiatrist only wants to "push meds," and that he's going to find someone else. You can spend ten minutes validating his feelings and recounting the experience. Or you can validate his feelings and explore how his frustration with his psychiatrist mimics other frustrations he's had with helping professionals. Which path would be more helpful?

Of course, there are some exceptions to this suggestion. Sometimes it's necessary to focus on details. For example, when a client discloses trauma, it can be helpful to understand the series of events.

If we're assessing for a diagnosis, it's essential to obtain relevant background information. But even when the details matter, it's often the patterns that matter more.

Most Unwanted Behaviors Are Solutions for Pain

I worked with a client who was referred to me for her raging cocaine and self-harm habit. Her therapy goals were simple and straightforward—she needed to significantly reduce or eliminate these destructive behaviors.

Here's what happened: After our first session together, she quit both habits for good. First session. No, I am not a therapist wizard holding the secret cure of addiction. This client had been in therapy for years—she had been to several treatment centers and she had stopped and started her drug and self-harm habit many times. I just happened to meet with her when she finally felt ready to make a positive change.

Despite achieving these impressive goals, my client still felt preoccupied with anxiety, shame, and low self-esteem. Although she had quit the dangerous habits, she didn't feel emotionally better. She frequently told me how she felt worse.

Many maladaptive behaviors are attempts to solve other problems. Her cocaine use and self-harm weren't the core issues. They were attempts to solve her pain—they helped numb the uncomfortable and intolerable emotions living deep inside her. Over time, when she began looking inward, she recognized her need to belong and feel loved. And that caused her pain. She had sought, and found, relief from the pain in using cocaine and self-harming.

Most clients want to focus on changing their undesirable behaviors. And we are quick to meet them there. Undesirable behaviors are tangible and concrete. Usually, we can quantify and measure them. We can plug them into a treatment plan and pat ourselves on the back when we see that the client has reduced their intensity or frequency.

But people trade behaviors all the time. They quit the cocaine and gamble instead. They stop the self-harm but throw themselves into compulsive exercise. They applaud themselves for making healthier and wiser choices, and we celebrate those successes with them.

We can all agree that some behaviors are more detrimental than others. And most therapists recognize harm reduction as a viable treatment approach over pure abstinence.

But we must also explore the concealed problems lying underneath the obvious problems. So, ask yourself, what's the actual issue? Why does the person need to engage in these maladaptive behaviors? Without these behaviors, what's really left?

Whatever is left is the work.

Conceptualize How Others May Perceive Your Client

I worked with a client who frequently complained about her brother's shallow behavior. By all means, his behavior sounded appalling. When they were young children, he had lit her dolls on fire. As teenagers, he had slept with her best friend and then dumped her the next day. He never called my client on her birthday. She insisted he cared more about money and status than family and friends. She called him an asshole, and I agreed with her insult. He did sound like an asshole.

But jumping to such conclusions is too straightforward and one-dimensional, and it doesn't account for the nuances of human behavior. It also doesn't benefit our clients. We must think systemically, and we must consider the role our clients play in their relationships. We need to account for their biases, and we should identify how their personalities impact other people.

What was my client not sharing about her brother? Even if he destroyed her dolls, did she ever destroy his? And what did she not understand about her brother? Although he had dumped her best friend, was it because he had felt guilty over his actions? Was he a genuine asshole?

Or did asshole just seem like the most fitting word to describe her frustration and hurt? Had she ever considered the role she played in their dynamic? If her brother could tell me his side of the story, what would he say? How would he defend his choices? And how did my countertransference affect the reality I chose to see?

This vignette isn't meant to negate my client's experiences. Her feelings were entirely real. My analysis of this vignette simply highlights the power of perspective. We all carry different biases and expectations for how people should behave.

Another time, I worked with a good-looking man who expressed persistent feelings of loneliness. After years in an unhappy, sexless marriage, he divorced his wife. Now he wanted to find companionship, and he couldn't understand why he struggled to date after his divorce. Although he went out with many "beautiful women," they typically lost interest after just a few dates. He couldn't understand why. He was in good shape, had a lucrative career, and he even had a puppy.

At first, I felt confused with him. How could such a charming, put-together person struggle so much? He was attractive and wealthy—shouldn't he have his pick of potential partners? When I expressed my confusion to my supervisor, she asked me to reflect on how he made me feel as a woman myself.

It was only then that I tapped into my own sense of discomfort with him. I recalled the story where he offended a date after telling her that her job sounded "adorable." I thought about his very graphic stories about sex and how he told me he felt disgusted when he looked at stretch marks and cellulite. I honed in on the time he asked me if I was single.

I had mistaken his crass attitude toward women as him just being brutally honest in therapy. But when I allowed myself to reflect on my feelings, I identified that I felt somewhat uncomfortable and frustrated. I imagined the other women must have felt as I did. If you're not sure how others might perceive your client, try to answer the following questions:

- What was your first impression of the client?

- What most annoys you about your client?

- What kind of person is most likely to be their enemy?

- What kind of person is most likely to be their best friend?

Integrate Collateral Information When Appropriate

Releases of information can provide invaluable information about our clients. How does the teacher or principal understand your depressed elementary-school client? How does the support staff observe your residential client? What significant history can parents, spouses, psychiatrists, or primary care physicians offer?

Do our clients act consistently with everyone, or do they act wildly different with some people? When integrating collateral information, notice the discrepancies in opinions or concerns. We tend to see the best in our clients (as we should). But we don't do ourselves or our clients any favors by not gathering the necessary information to understand their full behavioral picture.

Eliminate the Notion of Symptom-Free

Before my first-ever therapy session as a client, I held a lovely fantasy about therapy being this mystical, elusive experience. I imagined myself in the charming and dimly lit space, and I pictured myself revealing all the fragments of my self to an all-knowing mind reader. I'd feel safe from the first moment. I'd cry, and it would feel cathartic. She would listen compassionately before offering me the magical answer that would solve my distress.

Here's what really happened: During the intake session, when she asked what brought me to therapy, I rambled about a recent argument with one of my friends. I spent the next fifty minutes avoiding and downplaying anything resembling a genuine struggle. Although I hoped for some brilliant insight, she only prodded me with questions that made me feel even more insecure and uncertain. She was a skilled therapist, but I left the session convinced that therapy was a sham. I didn't feel fixed. What kind of shoddy business was this?

I still struggle with wanting to be symptom-free in my own life. After all, who wants to feel depressed or anxious? But if we are going to discuss symptoms, we must address the overarching scope of mental illness. Mental illness is chronic. There are no cures. We can aim for symptom management and periods of remission, but symptom-free just isn't a viable goal.

Ideally, we help reduce the severity of client symptoms. We teach them how to thrive despite their conditions. We accomplish this in many ways, including:

- helping them gain insight into problematic behaviors.

- teaching coping skills related to emotional regulation.

- helping them to improve the quality of their relationships.

- encouraging additional support and treatment.

We work with the conditions, not against them. We also advocate for acceptance. Acceptance isn't a free pass for ongoing distress or self-destruction. Acceptance means embracing mental illness for what it is—messy, imperfect, but not impossible to treat. We help our clients release unrealistic expectations of themselves. We teach them how to move away from self-loathing and resentments.

That said, perfection doesn't exist, and symptom-free is a form of perfection. Holding on to this misconception only perpetuates a dangerous mental health stigma.

Redefine Resistance

How many times have you called a client "resistant?" What does that word actually mean to you, and what prompts you to say it? In my experience, therapists often use resistance to describe any scenario when a client doesn't do what they want them to do. Thus, resistance is derogatory. It highlights that a client is "making things difficult."

But to really understand resistance, we must understand the delicate nature of psychotherapy. For one, being vulnerable is hard. It's really, really, really hard. Even when our clients want to reveal themselves, this desire doesn't necessarily make the daunting task easier. Second, who made us so important? Why should we assume our clients owe us anything? And if they do, why should it be on our terms?

We also confuse mistrust with resistance. Trust takes time, more time than we often want to admit. Trust requires passing certain emotional tests, and sometimes our clients don't know what these tests are until we pass them. Trust isn't a destination; we must cultivate and maintain it in every interaction we have with our clients. Therefore, we can't write the timeline for "Ct. will trust therapist" into a treatment plan. We can't quantify the meaning of it into an objective or goal. Trust is fluid; it takes time for it to manifest, and each client comes with unique barriers that may block it altogether. Instead of jumping to label resistance, consider asking yourself the following questions:

- What's preventing this client from feeling safe right now?

- Who made vulnerability dangerous for them?

- How can I provide compassion and guidance in this very moment?

I also recommend eliminating the word resistance from your therapist vocabulary. I did this during my second year of training. I just stopped using the term when talking about client behavior. As a result, the way I conducted therapy profoundly changed. I no longer felt so frustrated with particular clients. Rather than shame their behaviors, I felt more empathic and curious to understand what was really going on.

I discovered that resistance is usually just another word for fear. And when I could identify and dive into that fear, I could be a better therapist.

CHAPTER 5:

HOW TO BE A BETTER THERAPIST WHEN YOU STILL FEEL CLUELESS

New therapists aren't the only ones who feel insecure in their work. Maybe you've been in the field for years, and you still feel completely inept. Don't worry! I feel the same way, but I still have some tips that may help.

Understand Why the Concept of Theory Scares You

Theory often scares new therapists because they associate it like it's this all-or-nothing concept. I know I once thought this way. I assumed that I needed to master the concept of theory and perform its techniques flawlessly. This mindset is absurd. Let's say you want to convert to a new religion. Do you attend a single service or read one book and consider yourself converted? Of course not. You dedicate time and effort to this process. You talk to people who know about that religion and can help you. In some religions, conversion can take years. In the meantime, you remain open-minded and curious about growth.

But many therapists expect themselves to be masters from the beginning. They want to be fluent in a theory and heal their clients with their brilliance. But they're at a preschool level of understanding. And as far as I know, four-year-olds can't skip twelve grades and jump into college when they only know their primary colors. Likewise, new therapists should not read a single book about theory and expect to become an instant expert.

Theory can also scare therapists because it may highlight a sense of incompetence. Unfortunately, many theory textbooks reinforce these insecurities. Authors write about theories like delicious dessert recipes: if we just do X, we can achieve Y, and our clients will do Z.

But, in session, doing X doesn't feel right. We forget our lines, or the intervention feels sloppy and forced. The client doesn't react the way the book told us they would. Then we question if that theory was the right choice, and we feel annoyed we spent $15.99 on that stupid book.

But remember when I said that books don't always tell the truth? Theory books don't talk about the many *years and years and years* clinicians spend crafting their skills. They don't show the middle part of learning and implementing. They only display the end result. But nobody starts at the end. If you do, you're a wizard, and you've certainly wasted your money on my silly book.

Learn the Difference Between Conceptualization and Intervention

Conceptualization refers to how we understand a client. When we conceptualize a case, we interpret our client's behaviors to assume how they might respond to certain stimuli. Conceptualizations are not facts. They are predictions, and we use those predictions to intervene with our clients. Intervention, therefore, refers to action. It's what we say or do with a client.

Many times, new therapists only focus on interventions. They feel flustered over what they think they need to do with a client. Indeed, what we "do" matters, but we need conceptualization skills to intervene effectively. Without proper conceptualization, our therapy often feels scattered and random. We do things without knowing why we do them. We lack a reliable roadmap for where we intend to lead the client. Subsequently, therapists who lack conceptualization skills may:

- try a "bunch of different things" in session to see what works.

- act like a different therapist with each client.

- consistently feel confused or surprised by their client's behaviors.

- struggle with predicting outcomes.

- feel disconnected from their clients.

- only focus on the client's direct actions or words.

- go to their supervisors with the helpless question, "What do I do?"

A client with bulimia shared that she had purged the day before our session. She didn't outright acknowledge feeling scared to tell me, but I could conceptualize that she probably felt afraid. She had a long history of people shaming her for her eating disorder. She exhibited perfectionistic tendencies, and I knew she felt embarrassed by her perceived lack of progress.

Based on this simple conceptualization, I knew to offer her a validating statement and praise her for her honesty. I shifted into a more open posture to convey a sense of safety and warmth. I thanked her for trusting me with her secret, and I moved into exploring the triggers that had led to her purging. Those actions were my interventions.

When therapists feel lost with clients, it's usually because they are only thinking about their interventions. They focus only on the action rather than the forces driving those actions. But we can't land interventions if we don't conceptualize our clients.

So, move away from asking, *What should I do with my client?* Consider the question, *How should I think about my client?*

Understand How to Adapt When You Can't Use Your Theory

We can't always use our preferred theories with clients. Sometimes agencies require therapists to use specific, evidence-based treatments. Likewise, certain interventions work better with some disorders than others. As therapists, we should adapt to what best supports our clients. However, this doesn't mean we have to abandon our theory. It just means we adjust how we fit our theory into treatment.

I've worked with many clients struggling with OCD, where exposure and response prevention (ERP) is currently the leading standard for treatment. Yet, I am psychodynamically oriented. How does that mismatch work?

It works because I know the difference between conceptualization and intervention. I may conceptualize where the OCD stems from—a history of trauma, a fear of abandonment, internalized anxiety. I might postulate how the client relies on their compulsions to mitigate distress or feel a semblance of control over their lives. I might even consider the transference piece: I notice when clients value my approval or want to please me with their progress. These conceptualization skills help me anticipate how our work might evolve.

If our time is limited, I won't spend it using free association, exploring transference, dream analysis, or other classic psychodynamic interventions. Instead, I'll rely on cognitive-behavioral exercises. I'll offer an exercise called a fear hierarchy with my client. We'll engage in exposure work to desensitize their debilitating fears. We'll discuss relaxation strategies, and we'll collaborate on homework designed to continue exposure throughout the week.

Flexibility is key. Remember that your theory often has less to do with how you act and more to do with how you think.

Stick to the Basics and Avoid Fuckarounditis

In the weightlifting world, *fuckarounditis* is a slang term for spending excess time in the gym without making meaningful progress. New lifters often walk around the gym haphazardly, hop on all the machines, and do whatever looks interesting. They might try a particular workout routine one day, and then they switch to something new a few days later. There isn't any real consistency. As a result, each session looks different, and the new lifter struggles to make progress.

Successful lifters, on the other hand, have an intention when they exercise. They know what they're going to do that day. Their workouts usually consist of compound power moves like squats, deadlifts, overhead shoulder presses, push-ups, and pull-ups. They work on these same moves in every session for years. They watch tutorials and check their form, and they progressively add weight to each exercise when it's appropriate.

As therapists, our compound power moves consist of warmth, active listening, unconditional positive regard, and critical thinking. With these moves, we can do nearly anything in our sessions. We can handle almost anything a client brings to us.

But many therapists get lost in the therapy gym. They come to sessions lacking a plan, and they try everything to see what works best. They jump on the treadmill for ten minutes, and then they're doing bicep curls and lunges. Then they see someone else on the rowing machine, so they give that a try. This strategy isn't wrong. You are, after all, doing something. But it often feels sloppy because there isn't a structure or routine. Some therapists might know how to do a hundred interventions, but they don't know how to do any of them very well. It's no wonder their clients don't progress much.

Don't lose sight of the basic components that make for good therapy. You have power moves—use them. Don't get lost in fuckarounditis. Therapy isn't just about what you learn from fancy conferences, training manuals, or treatment planning. If you focus on the basics and practice doing them as well as possible, the rest of therapy tends to fall into place.

Eclectic Isn't a Curse Word

We aren't locked into our therapeutic styles. Sometimes, our mindset changes over time. Maybe we learn about a new theory, and that one makes more sense. Perhaps we start working with a new population or disorder, and we realize we need to expand our skills.

Fuckarounditis refers to performing numerous exercises without any real plan or structure. Despite the harsh name, fuckarounditis isn't actually dangerous. If you want to exercise for the sake of being healthy and active, you don't need to follow an overly specific plan. But if you're trying to achieve particular results, having a plan certainly helps. Knowing what works reduces the risk of wasting time, money, and unnecessary strain on your body.

I would argue that the same philosophy applies to theory. It's okay if you want to keep things eclectic. It's okay to dip into Gestalt techniques with some clients and CBT with others. As I highlighted with my OCD example, we don't always conceptualize in the same theory as we intervene. But we need to know how these techniques work—we can't just borrow from them without understanding their merit. Get out of the habit of trying interventions for the sake of trying them. Instead, move into the mindset of being able to own why you choose to do what you do with a client.

There's nothing wrong with practicing from an eclectic framework. I actually believe true eclectic therapists often work harder than therapists who operate from a single theory. They need to be flexible and responsive to different styles, and they need to have a breadth of knowledge in various theories.

But being eclectic doesn't mean stumbling around and finding what works. "Doing whatever" is not therapy. Individualizing and honing our approach for our client is therapy. If you want to be eclectic, be eclectic! To some extent, most of us are in our practice. Just don't lose sight of the importance of theory. Being an "eclectic" therapist shouldn't be a rationalization for trying out new interventions. Instead, doing what's in the best interest of the client should be the rationalization.

Acknowledge When You Don't Know Something

Clients ask us all sorts of questions: *Can I drink alcohol if I'm taking Prozac? Should I break up with my boyfriend? Is my car a tax write-off? Does the restaurant next door have good Thai food? What actually causes depression?*

Clients ask us questions for many reasons. Sometimes they don't understand the scope of our expertise; they assume we can provide medical, legal, or financial advice. Other times they're curious about our opinions because they value what we have to say. And sometimes, even when they have a legitimate question related to therapy, we don't have the answer. Get in the habit of acknowledging your uncertainty by saying:

- I don't know, but I'm happy to find out for you!

- That's an excellent question. I don't have a clue. What do you think?

- I don't know, but maybe we can talk about it together.

- I don't know, and I'm wondering what triggered you to ask that?

- I don't know, and it's actually not in my scope to provide you with that kind of information.

Some clinicians want to explore the meaning behind each question a client asks. I can respect this approach, as the answers may reveal telling information. But sometimes a question is just a question. Sometimes a client is just really hungry, and they're debating between tacos or Thai food, and they value your essential input on the fried rice.

Whatever you do, don't pretend you know the answer to sound smart or impressive. If you haven't tried the Thai place, don't say you have. You might get away with lying, but it's disingenuous and uncomfortable. Additionally, our clients are smart, and they might figure out this deception.

When we can admit we don't have an answer, we model humility. Demonstrating humility helps build trust, as it displays the human side of our personality. We show our clients that imperfection is okay. Most importantly, we release personal responsibility if they choose to eat tacos.

Learn How Transference Actually Works

Have you ever been in love with a therapist? At one point in my life, I thought I was. My therapist made me feel safe, supported, and special in ways nobody else had before. Every week, my feelings intensified. They gnawed at me. I desperately longed for us to be friends. I didn't know what transference was then. I just thought I was crazy for how I felt.

Transference happens when our clients redirect and apply feelings or expectations onto us. For example, if we remind them of their mother, they may seek our approval and love. If they feel attracted to us, they might talk more candidly about sex and intimacy or make overt sexual comments in our session. Transference can be complicated because it's rooted in emotional memories instead of logic. We may look or act nothing like their mothers, but something about us evokes an experience of what they had or didn't have.

Sometimes we're the only people who listen to our clients. We display a genuine curiosity in who they are instead of what they do or what they offer. We believe in their courage; we validate their feelings; we tell them it's okay to unravel. Transference can amplify our compassion; it can place us on impossible pedestals where our clients think we're perfect and infallible.

At the same time, transference can be painful for clients. It can cause them to feel obsessed with us. It can result in them feeling distracted by our presence—they become focused on what we think, rather than what they need.

As therapists, we will make mistakes. We unintentionally dismiss their experiences. We double-book sessions. We forget to follow up on a topic that might have upset them the previous week. Transference can make our minor mistakes feel catastrophic to the client. It can leave our clients feeling betrayed, abandoned, and resentful.

But how do you know when a client is experiencing transference? Usually, the signs are subtle. Pay attention to when a client seemingly idolizes you. Idolization can look like excessive compliments or hanging on your every word. *Nobody else understands me like you do. I always feel safe talking to you.*

It can also take the form of subjective statements about how they imagine you in your personal life. *You must be a great mom. I bet your house is so clean. All your friends must absolutely love you.* You also need to pay attention to when a client feels angry at you. *You only listen to me because I'm paying you. You probably just think I'm stupid.*

Ultimately, how you deal with transference depends on what theories you draw on. For now, it's essential to remember that transference exists, it's important, and you need to identify when it's happening.

Learn How Countertransference Actually Works

I have a thin tolerance for so many things: Lukewarm coffee. Drivers who refuse to use turn signals. Mayonnaise. People who misuse the term *countertransference.*

Countertransference refers to the feelings we transfer onto our clients. It's how we project our realities onto the people we treat. I could write on and on about countertransference, but many other professionals have already done a fantastic job in explaining this concept.

The founder of the Psychiatry & Psychotherapy Podcast, David Puder, MD, shared a checklist he uses to screen his countertransference when working with clients. He assesses seven basic emotions to check in with his feelings, and I love how he breaks them down. With his permission, I've taken his concept and applied some of my own reactions that I've felt toward clients.

Disgust

- I dislike this client.

- I feel repulsed by what they just said.

- I can't believe they actually did that.

Attraction and Affection

- If this was not my client, I would want to date them.

- I feel distracted by my attractive client.

- I want to have sex with my client.

- I feel like I understand my client more than anyone else.

- I have warm feelings toward my client.

- I want to protect my client like they're my child.

- I really enjoy our sessions together.

Sadness

- I feel sad about what has happened to this client.

- I feel depressed after our sessions.

- I am upset with other people for hurting my client.

Anger

- I feel annoyed by my client's decisions.

- I feel angry at the other people in my client's life.

- I'm feeling used or manipulated by my client.

- I want to hurt my client.

- I feel competitive with my client.

Dissociation:

- I feel confused about what's going on with my client.

- I feel a sense of hopelessness in how I can help this client.

- My emotions are overwhelming in this session.

Sensorium issues:

- I can't stay focused in our sessions.

- I feel bored with this client.

- I am thinking about a million other things right now.

Anxiety:

- I feel nervous in our sessions.

- I doubt my own skills with this client.

- I wonder what judgments this client has about me.

- I feel uncomfortable when my client talks about that topic.

- I feel incompetent when trying to help.

- I worry about my client excessively between sessions.

Many therapists wrongfully assume that countertransference is bad. It isn't. It's entirely normal, and it isn't something we need to overcome or fix. If anything, it holds the roadmap to helping our clients heal. However, we must also be aware of our countertransference. Without such awareness, we risk stunting our therapy and even harming our clients.

For years, I struggled with working with middle-aged clients. As I previously mentioned, I was the youngest student in my cohort, and I struggled with feeling inferior about my age. To me, my education paled in comparison to their many years of enriching life experience. As a child, I had sought approval from my parents. As a young therapist, I experienced this same pattern with my older clients. I wanted to prove my worth, and I often acted more submissively in an effort to please. I avoided confrontation. I dressed more conservatively, used more clinical terms, and I definitely steered away from saying "fuck." After my husband proposed, I loved wearing my engagement ring at work, as if my new piece of jewelry signified my maturity. Were my reactions wrong? Not necessarily. And maybe not at all. But my countertransference may have pivoted the sessions in ways that fulfilled my needs instead of theirs.

A colleague and I were recently discussing her struggles with countertransference. She was working with a young woman who went to a bar, drank too much, and left with an equally drunk stranger. The client reported that she believed this stranger had pressured her into having sex. However, she also emphasized the details were fuzzy—she couldn't recall the exact sequence of events the next morning. My colleague felt sad and protective of her client. She also felt a surge of anger toward the stranger.

As it turns out, my colleague had unprocessed emotions related to past sexual trauma. As a result, after the client's disclosure, she had quickly insisted that this incident was a huge deal, even though the client shrugged it off. She labeled it as rape, but the client called it a bad, drunken night. My colleague shared about encouraging her client to call the police and file a report. The client told her that action seemed excessive.

I'm not suggesting that my colleague acted inappropriately. But when we aren't aware of our countertransference, we risk overreacting or underreacting. We risk missing what our client needs from us because we're busy thinking about what we need instead.

Countertransference isn't always about our own unprocessed experiences. Sometimes, we feel countertransference when we have emotional reactions that don't quite feel like our own. For instance, you ask your client about a recent stressor at their job. They respond appropriately, but you feel a tightness in your chest as they talk. There appears to be no reason for you to have this physiological reaction. The material wasn't triggering, the conversation wasn't particularly deep, and yet, the feeling overwhelms you. What's going on? Chances are, your client is having a conscious or unconscious reaction, and they're projecting those emotions onto you. Therefore, you're subconsciously having a reaction to this dynamic, almost on their behalf.

Remember that countertransference is the compass that guides our reactions and interventions. If we lack insight into what's going on with us, we may treat our clients in ways that attempt to heal our own experiences rather than being available to help them heal. In other cases, we avoid dealing with the issues altogether. We move around the discomfort and focus on something else.

Experiment with Self-Disclosure

The more I learned about countertransference, the more I began placing value on my feelings in the therapy room. As I discussed previously, our feelings about our clients often mimic how others feel about our clients. Sharing these feelings, along with sharing other parts of ourselves, can deepen the therapeutic process profoundly.

However, self-disclosure is tricky, and many therapists misuse or even abuse it. When abused, it is unproductive, and it can damage the therapeutic relationship.

My favorite professor held a firm stance against self-disclosure. In my first year of training, I followed his guidance and withheld almost all personal information from my clients. With my first clients, I attempted to act like a stoic ice queen. Unfortunately, I just wasn't icy enough. When a client asked me where I went to school, I panicked. If someone asked me how my day was going, I diverted the question awkwardly. I didn't feel skilled enough to resort to the more psychoanalytic approach of saying, "I wonder why it's important for you to know how my day is going." Instead, I just spent a lot of time skirting around talking about myself.

The shift into finding my groove with self-disclosure took time. I listened to how my colleagues used it in supervision. I thought about the instances when I find self-disclosure helpful as a client. In my practice, I first experimented with calculated snippets. A stressed mother of three asked if I had my own children. At the time, that was an easy no. Another client wanted to know if I had ever struggled with addiction. That was also a no. Someone else wanted to know why I became a therapist. I responded that I wanted to help people.

I watched how clients reacted to my self-disclosure. Many of them felt reassured. Some of them told me it helped them feel more understood or connected. Others worried I couldn't help them, but this fear offered rich material for our therapy process.

Of course, we must be careful with our self-disclosure, and I believe in erring on the side of caution. You can't take back what you say, and you can't control what your client does with the information you give them. Most therapists recommend only self-disclosing if the disclosure benefits the client. I argue that we need to refine this concept even further. It's not just about if self-disclosure benefits a client. It's about *how* it benefits them. Will it help strengthen rapport? Help them feel less alone? Encourage them to take that risk they've wanted to take? In my practice, if I can't answer how self-disclosure will help someone, I know it's not the right moment. While we probably can't underdo talking about ourselves, we can certainly overdo it.

Not all therapists use self-disclosure. That's okay—the decision is yours. Similarly, you may feel more comfortable disclosing with some clients but not others. If you're a therapist in training, consider consulting with your supervisor if you need guidance. Just remember, after we strip away the professional titles and remove the clinical jargon, we're only human beings. And it's perfectly normal for our clients to be curious about the lives we live.

Be Mindful of Working with Clients Who Share Your Same Issues

Many therapists with personal histories of certain issues want to specialize in helping clients struggling with the same problem. I have noticed this trend when working with eating disorders and substance use disorders. However, it exists everywhere in mental health.

Therapists who want to work with clients like themselves have good intentions. Sometimes, they want to give back what they've received. Or they hope to be the advocate they never had. Equipped with first-hand knowledge, they believe they can understand their clients in ways other therapists cannot. But let's discuss some potential roadblocks.

Countertransference

I discussed countertransference and how to identify its impact on your work as a therapist. When you are working with someone who has similar issues as you, you're incredibly susceptible to experiencing intense countertransference. Some examples of this include:

- overly identifying with the client's experience.

- struggling to maintain objectivity because you believe certain treatment models or interventions are better or worse than others.

- having difficulty meeting the client at their current state because you feel desperate to address themes of denial or minimization.

- taking the client's progress or lack of progress personally.

Unresolved Personal Recovery

Recovery is a complex concept, and everyone defines it differently. Yet many therapists enter the field with unresolved issues related to their mental health. They then gravitate toward treating people like themselves.

They hope their treatment can inadvertently heal their own struggles. However, this method is rarely sustainable. Often, these therapists find themselves sharing advice that they themselves aren't taking. They might present as knowledgeable and stable at work, but some clients may notice the discrepancies. The individual recovering from substance abuse notices the therapist's slightly dilated pupils. The client with the eating disorder observes the therapist's changes in weight. And even if they don't observe your struggles, do you really want to live with such dishonesty?

Risk for Relapse

I have known several therapists who have struggled in their own recoveries while working with a specific population. I don't believe they were doomed, and I also don't think relapse is inevitable. But relapse among therapists working with clients who share their same struggles can happen because:

- You take on the emotional stress associated with working with such clients.

- You spend the majority of your working day talking about the condition, which can trigger cravings.

- You constantly spend your days normalizing and validating relapse, which can inadvertently convince you that it's not a big deal.

Challenges with Self-Disclosure

When I worked in substance abuse treatment, many of my colleagues had personal histories with addiction. They frequently shared about their experiences with clients. Some clients admired the staff for their bravery and often perceived them as role models. However, some clients felt annoyed and uncomfortable. They complained about their therapists' excessive self-disclosure, and they argued that some staff had rigid expectations about what recovery should entail.

As therapists, where do we draw these complicated lines? Is it appropriate to share the darkest despairs of our own journeys? If a client is struggling, is it reasonable to talk about how we personally relate to their experience? How do we maintain a neutral and open-minded approach if we believe one treatment method is superior to others?

Additional Considerations

Therapists with sustained recovery can provide excellent treatment for their clients. But I believe prospective therapists who wish to work with such clients must be:

- actively involved in personal therapy.

- highly cognizant of relapse behaviors and have a relapse prevention plan.

- willing to do any extra work needed to identify countertransference issues.

- working closely with a knowledgeable and attuned supervisor.

- connected with strong peer supports.

- aware of their own inherent limitations as a therapist.

When You Lose Your Empathy, Localize the Pain

We're all going to have challenging clients. They might be boring, frustrating, sociopathic, narcissistic, or oozing with a victim mentality. If you haven't had one of those clients yet, you will. You won't like everyone who enters your office. At times, you may even feel like you hate specific clients. Being attuned to your countertransference can help you keep your emotions and reactions in check.

Therapists aren't perfect. We become impatient and agitated. We become distracted and wish we were at the beach or eating lunch. We find ourselves judging our clients and making quick assumptions about their feelings or behavior. Some of these reactions come from countertransference. Others come from the numerous distractions that impact us during our sessions.

We always need to pay special attention when we find ourselves losing empathy. If therapy is a house, trust is the foundation, and empathy lies within the walls. A lack of empathy is a countertransference problem, but it's also a practical problem. When we lose empathy, we risk becoming resentful, making unfair assumptions, judging our clients, and taking shortcuts in our work.

All voluntary clients enter therapy because they are in some kind of pain. Sometimes their pain is apparent. They know it, and we know it, and we can work through it without much digging. But other times, the pain exists in covert layers. People conceal their damage in all kinds of ways. They lie and omit, they suppress and rationalize, they dress themselves in classy clothes and makeup, or they bury it under alcohol and substances. All pain hurts, and we are wired to avoid hurt.

I like inner-child work, and when I find myself losing empathy for a client, I imagine them as a small child, around three years old. I am patient and understanding with children. I don't blame them for their distress, and I don't feel frustrated or judgmental of their behavior. In my opinion, children are perfectly innocent—they are just products of their circumstances. Many of our clients are wounded children in adult bodies. They move through life wanting love and freedom and happiness, but they don't know how to get those things.

When we lose empathy, we must focus on what I call *localizing the pain*. Think about where it hurts, and think about why it hurts. Imagine your client as a three-year-old who needs your love, attention, and patience. Imagine them as a young child who feels abandoned or scared.

Aim to Remember the Obscure Details

As therapists, we have to remember *a lot* of client information. We might see several clients each day, and we juggle different names and presenting problems and complicated life stories. But genuine connection exists beyond knowing this basic information. It exists within the small, intimate details.

Some of my clients think I have an incredible memory. They're not entirely wrong—I have the blessing, or curse, of remembering useless facts and insignificant dialogues from over a decade ago. But if you can remember an arbitrary detail from your client's story, they will also assume you have a fantastic memory.

Of course, it's expected that you remember crucial details like the fact that your client has depression and is going through a painful breakup. But when you remember that her sister is lactose intolerant and her mother is dating a new man named Steve, you convey your uncanny attentiveness to her life.

You showcase a skill that most of our clients rarely experience: active, compassionate, and detail-oriented listening.

Although the therapy goals matter, the therapeutic relationship matters even more. Our clients are not just the representations of their problems. They are whole people with whole lives and whole stories. Earlier, I recommended that you avoid getting lost in all the details, but that doesn't mean you shouldn't *listen* to the details. Pay attention to their boss's name or their favorite breakfast or where they traveled last summer. If you struggle with forgetfulness and know you won't remember this information, write down some of these facts after your session.

Of course, you must integrate this nuanced information appropriately. Nobody wants their therapist sounding like a weird stalker. But throwing in a specific detail once or twice can make a tremendous impact.

Understand That Shame Is Always Your Greatest Enemy

I love shame. I devour the works of Brené Brown and John Bradshaw like they are gourmet chocolates. Shame is as universal as it is private, as powerful as it is fragile. But we are all hyped up on shame lately, aren't we? It's the feeling of the decade, and I believe people flock to my Psychotherapy Memes community because I opt to display my shame, slice it with a cake knife, and offer everyone a piece.

Shame is the pulse of self-loathing, self-doubt, and self-defeating behaviors. Shame can keep us sick, but we often point to other people and places or circumstances as being the source. Because shame is painful and it's scary, and we don't quite know what to do with it.

As you sit with your clients, search for the shame. It's there. It's *always* there. Some of your clients will be aware of the shame and its function. Those clients have typically spent years in therapy, analyzing and assessing the details of their past. They will discuss shame like an entree on a menu; they've ordered it for dinner, and they'd like to share half of it with you.

But the majority of your clients won't understand their shame. They'll understand that they lack confidence or despise their spouse. They'll talk about their problems at work or the neighbor who plays his drums too loudly. They don't realize they walk around wearing shame like it's a trendy outfit. Shame will be the greatest barrier between you and most clients. That's because unprocessed shame can lead clients to:

- withhold essential information because they fear judgment and rejection.

- fabricate stories to cultivate a desired identity.

- use defense mechanisms to deflect from the here-and-now.

- terminate therapy prematurely.

But shame is subtle, and many therapists overlook it. Instead, they focus on the content. They focus on what's being said rather than consider what's *not* being said. They take details at face value. They don't investigate nearly enough.

How do you know when you've tapped in to shame? You feel the energy shift. A thickness sits in the air. The connection starts to feel strained. The client flounders. They start withdrawing, diverting, making jokes, or avoiding answering questions. They do whatever they can to restore homeostasis or maintain a sense of balance.

That is the shame. And the true shame isn't even the first or second recognition of shame someone might share. True shame often lies underneath the safer shame, hidden and concealed as if with a deadbolt lock. Maybe you'll reach it, but remember, this shame lives at the end of all the defenses. It's the final layer of vulnerability. True shame comes last. Always.

Successful Therapy Doesn't Mean Exciting Breakthroughs Occur in Every Session

Like all relationships, therapy has its ups and downs. Some sessions are intense and filled with gusto. Others seem more simplistic and mundane. Do not assume that emotionally charged sessions inherently have more value than lighter ones.

I remember an incredibly powerful session with one of my clients. She had finally spilled all the contents of the wrenching trauma that had been haunting her for decades. For weeks, we'd been dancing at the tip of this trauma. I knew she wanted to talk about it, but I also sensed her apprehension and fear. She sobbed as she shared her story. She then left our session by telling me she felt relieved to finally release her pain. She finally felt ready to dive into the work.

Afterward, I spent some time reflecting on the experience. I felt accomplished and proud of myself. I did it! I had made her feel safe and secure. She trusted me enough to reveal her innermost secrets, and I was going to help heal her wounds.

I felt so eager to meet with her again, so ready to plunge into the terrors plaguing her. At our next session, we assumed our usual positions. She flopped on the couch, and I sat upright in my chair. I leaned in, maintaining a gentle posture and a calm demeanor, and asked her how she was doing that day. *I'm safe*, I wanted to convey. *I'm so safe, and you know I'm safe, so let's get back to where we were.*

And she started talking about the traffic. The freeway construction was horrific, and someone in a Mercedes had cut her off on the way to my office. Next, she reported that her dog had eaten half a box of chocolate cookies and vomited all over her new loveseat. She'd had to spend almost a thousand dollars at the emergency vet to make sure he was okay. And there was construction on her way there!

I nodded. These events sounded stressful, and I recognized that she needed to vent about them for a moment. We'd get back to where we had ended the previous week, I thought. But she kept talking about the traffic.

I gently tried to draw attention to her avoidance. "We covered so much ground last week. I know it must have been so tough, but I felt so honored that you shared your story with me. I'm wondering how you felt after you left the office."

She looked down at her untied shoelaces. She shifted on the couch and ran a hand through her hair. Then she said, "I felt fine. I am feeling so distracted by all these other things that happened, anyway. I think I need to spend more time talking about them."

Most therapists would start berating themselves at this point. And I did exactly that. Where did I go wrong? Why didn't she want to continue with our trauma work? How was I going to pick up these scattered pieces? Had I pushed her too far? Should I keep prodding?

The truth is that emotions stretch and wane, and they all come with expiration dates. My client wasn't intentionally avoiding her emotions. Instead, at that moment, she was just in another space. A safer space where she felt more bothered by the current traffic than by her childhood memories of her parents beating her.

We can never forget that vulnerability is exhausting, and talking about trauma is both jarring and taxing. I've mentioned that progress doesn't move in a linear direction. Clients can feel safe one moment and entirely exposed the next. If not handled with care, a client's vulnerability can shatter entire therapy relationships. Have you ever labeled a cardboard box as fragile while packing for a move? How much did you really trust the movers to take extra precautions? You hoped for the best, but you also probably braced for the possibility of them breaking your beloved item. We must respect all steps our clients take toward expressing vulnerability. We must remember that many of them have experienced backlash because of revealing their vulnerability in the past.

Athletes understand that rest periods are just as crucial as workouts. Overexertion increases the likelihood for injury, and muscle growth occurs during the rest period. In therapy, we also need our rest periods. Too many intense sessions in a row can backfire. We all need time to rest and regroup.

Sometimes Our Job Is Just Highlighting Dynamics

Our clients come to us with their many defenses. They avoid responsibility. They sabotage themselves. They blame others for their misery. They keep repeating the same habits, and they don't know how to stop even when they want to stop.

As therapists, one of our most important goals is strengthening insight. Our goal isn't to fix patterns or give direct answers. Often, it's shining light onto unconscious patterns. It's pointing out how our client repeatedly asks us for coping skills, but then refuses to use them. It's telling a husband that you notice he looks away whenever his wife starts crying. It's teaching parents how their behavior impacts their child's behavior.

Although we should highlight patterns and dynamics with our clients, this doesn't always lead to change. We can offer tidbits and guidance, but our clients may cling to their habits out of an unconscious need for homeostasis. That's okay. Change is hard, and our clients don't owe us change.

Most of us have heard the term *planting the seed.* In good therapy, we plant seeds—even when our clients insist they don't have any room left in their gardens.

Understand the Reality of the Good-Enough Goodbye

I can't talk about good therapy without talking about termination. Termination can be one of the most challenging, painful parts of the therapeutic process.

In life, we don't prepare for goodbyes. When we like someone, we intend to see them again. When we don't like someone, we reduce or cut our contact altogether. Even when we encounter death—the ultimate goodbye, the one we all know is inevitable—we still experience a unique tornado of grief in reaction to the loss.

Therapy is one of the only intimate relationships people enter into with the intention of it ending. In an ideal world, our work concludes when the client meets their treatment goals. But termination doesn't always happen under these optimal conditions. Many times, someone or something else dictates termination, including:

- insurance or specific workplace constraints.

- monetary issues necessitate the need to refer elsewhere.

- the client or therapist moving to a new location.

- the therapist changing jobs.

- the client discontinues therapy on their own and avoiding further contact.

Each of these barriers can trigger difficult feelings for both the client and the therapist. We feel frustrated when we feel cheated of having a proper goodbye. We worry about our client's safety and well-being. There isn't a simple solution to these painful experiences. Sometimes we just need to endure them.

But if you have the opportunity to plan and prepare for a goodbye, consider how you intend to structure it. We owe it to our clients to model healthy closure. The first and most important step is talking about termination. Don't wait to talk about it in the last or second-to-last session to have this discussion. Depending on the client, you might want to broach the subject at least a month or so in advance. Long-term clients may require more notice.

Share your fears or reactions honestly. It's okay to acknowledge your discomfort, and it's reasonable to share your feelings about your therapeutic relationship. This modeling lays the initial groundwork for healthy emotional expression. It provides permission for clients to share their feelings with you.

Clients react in all kinds of ways to planned terminations. Some openly describe their feelings, but many don't. Clients often feel self-conscious about coming across as needy, dependent, or scared. As a result, they might seem completely unfazed by ending your work together. Many therapists feel confused or even offended when this happens. You might question the effectiveness of your therapy, the rapport you have with your client, or the progress you thought you made leading to termination.

If these feelings arise, you might want to lean into your conceptualization. From your therapeutic perspective, what do you know about your client? What have you learned about them from past interactions that you can now apply to better understand their current behavior? What discrepancies do you notice? Does anything seem out of line with this goodbye?

Pay attention to any shifts over the next few sessions. Clients who feel anxious, bothered, or afraid of termination often show slight changes. They might withdraw from you, regress in certain behaviors, begin asking more personal questions, or cancel and reschedule sessions. They might also bring up a new presenting problem or reject your referrals to other therapists. Most clients will deny these behaviors or rationalize them. That's okay. It can be a fantastic opportunity to identify how their termination reactions relate to other patterns in their life.

We often associate a healthy goodbye as if it's a happily-ever-after ending in a movie. We place intense expectations about how we need to act and how they need to respond. But, in reality, goodbyes can be disruptive and untimely. They can be painful for everyone. Terminations aren't movie scripts.

Our clients are not curated characters with curated feelings. We don't get perfect endings when we end a relationship. But that doesn't mean our clients haven't grown or learned from the experience.

At times, I offer transitional objects to clients when termination is particularly difficult. These objects are meant to be comforting and soothing—I intend for them to support my client after our work concludes.

I don't believe one object is better than another. When I worked with children, I often gave them dolls, stuffed animals, or toys. I've given adult clients items like journals, books, blankets, and stones. I usually pair these objects with a brief letter describing how I felt about our work. I include my perceptions about their progress, hopes for their future, and any lessons they have taught me. As I have always expressed myself with writing, I value sharing my reactions in such an intimate and concrete way. If clients reach out to me after our work, they often reference that letter.

Terminations are undoubtedly hard. But as therapists, we have a unique role in modeling a healthy closure. Try to honor this role as best you can.

Write Down One Success and One Struggle After Every Session

Looking back, I wish I had done this exercise when I first started my practicum. But I wasn't as brilliant then as I am now. This one-minute habit can be so beneficial for your career growth. First, it's a generous act of self-compassion to acknowledge your successes. Most of us are much too hard on ourselves. Second, understanding your patterns of success increases your insight into your therapeutic strengths.

Some successes will feel obvious. Other times, they may require more digging. During particularly rough sessions, those successes may feel small and insignificant, especially if you stack them next to your struggles. Write them down anyway.

Similarly, some struggles will also feel obvious. Notice I am not using the word failure. Failure is harsh; it's dramatic, and it's shame-based. If you're not having sex with clients, abusing them, or illegally breaking their confidentiality, there's a good chance you're not failing. Identify a struggle in each session, but just choose one.

Do this exercise after meeting with every client. What trends do you observe? What successes do you keep repeating? Do you continue to have similar struggles each day, or do they vary from client to client? Most importantly, how can you grow from these struggles?

CHAPTER 6:

HOW TO SUCCEED IN THE WORKPLACE AND WIN EMPLOYEE OF THE YEAR

My graduate school prepared me to work with the ideal client—the motivated, middle-class adult with above-average insight. As a training therapist, I looked forward to the long-term, in-depth work. I anticipated crushing the therapy scene—getting my hands dirty and solving existential crises. My clients would gossip to their friends about my impressive sorcery over brunch cocktails. They would reference my expertise in their best-selling memoirs.

Imagine my surprise when my first client sat before me, stared at her chipped nails, and said, "Yeah, I don't really know why I'm here. I hate therapists." Then, imagine my disdain when I tried to process and validate her feelings, and she never came back.

Many of us begin our practices working in agencies with clients who don't really know what they need and who don't stick around for very long. We often don't feel prepared for this kind of work. Some agencies can be disorganized and full of bureaucracy complications. It can be frustrating to have many no-shows and deal with back-to-back meetings. Sometimes, we spend the bulk of our time playing phone tag and tackling endless piles of paperwork. We may take on enormous and unmanageable caseloads. We may use supply closets, empty classrooms, basketball courts, or garages as our makeshift offices. Then, we have to listen to people kindly reminding us that we're lucky to receive a paycheck.

That said, there are many advantages to these settings. Agency work exposes us to a variety of clients with many different backgrounds. Agencies teach therapists how to be flexible and think quickly and critically—we learn to make the most out of our time with clients. We can enjoy the valuable benefit of collaborating and coordinating care with other professionals. Finally, we don't need to worry about marketing ourselves, leasing an office space, or calculating whether we will earn enough money to pay this month's rent.

Understand the Key Differences Between Private Practice and Every Other Clinical Setting

Because my graduate education focused on working in private practice, I struggled during my first few months working in an agency. I didn't know terminations could be so abrupt; I didn't realize some organizations expected therapists to do more than therapy.

Today, I understand the types of work are profoundly different. But I know many novice therapists don't feel prepared for agency work. Let's review the differences.

Long-term vs. Short-term Therapy

Many agencies specialize in providing short-term therapy to clients. This is due to a variety of factors: organizational funding, insurance restrictions, long waitlists, and specific company policies. Instead of spending months building rapport with a client, you may have approval for only four sessions.

With that in mind, I recommend that all therapists gain experience in short-term therapy. This kind of work forces you to get to the point. You must prioritize every moment of your treatment—you learn to shape your therapy to focus on the most pressing issues without wasting time. Likewise, some clients *prefer* this method. They don't want to spend years in therapy. As therapists, we should honor this need.

Of course, short-term work isn't exclusive to agencies. Many therapists in their own practice meet with clients for just a few sessions. This could also be due to insurance authorization constraints. However, some therapists prefer using short-term models. That said, private-practice therapists typically have much more freedom in determining how long they work with a client.

Caseloads

Productivity is an important component of succeeding in agency work. At times, the push for productivity supersedes personal comfort, but this is a sign of a toxic work environment, which I'll discuss later in the book.

In an agency, you may have many clients on your caseload. This isn't inherently a bad thing, particularly if you are a new therapist. The continuous exposure to working with different people is so crucial for growing your skills. That said, it's no secret that exceptionally high caseloads can feel grueling and exhaustive.

In private practice, the therapist controls the caseload. This freedom can be a tremendous benefit (when things are going well), and a terrifying reality (when you're struggling to obtain clients). Most therapists consider "full time" as twenty to thirty clients per week. Of course, this number fluctuates based on the therapist's comfort, hours desired to work, and fees.

Scope of Competence

Some agencies struggle with chronic staffing and funding problems. Client screening processes—if they even exist— might be minimal. For this reason, many therapists teeter on the potentially unethical line of working out of their scope of competence. Sometimes, if a therapist expresses concern about this, their director or supervisor may balk at the idea of transferring the client to a different therapist or not offering treatment at all. This reality can place agency therapists in a difficult position. They want to provide the best care for their clients without causing disturbances in the workplace.

In private practice, therapists can be as thorough as they want during the screening process. They can ensure they treat only clients with specific issues, and they can refer people to another professional without seeking permission.

Having Multiple Roles

Agency-based therapists rarely provide just therapy. They may be responsible for administrative tasks, screening intakes, coordinating referrals, and case management. I believe each of these skills is essential, and I feel grateful for my experiences in learning them. That said, my school didn't prepare me to take on these roles, and I felt utterly confused when my first boss asked me to do something outside of my therapy wheelhouse.

At times, balancing multiple roles can create issues with boundaries and dual relationships. Having excess responsibilities is also tedious and time-consuming, and these factors can cause burnout. Agency therapists should be aware of these risks and address them throughout their work. If you're asked to do a job that you don't know how to do, it's time for a conversation with your supervisor.

In private practice, therapists work as therapists. While some take on other roles or responsibilities by choice, the primary focus lies in providing therapy.

Being "with" Clients

In milieu-based settings like schools, hospitals, residential facilities, or prisons, therapists see their clients and interact with them outside of therapy sessions. As a result, the relationship is different. The clients sometimes want to eat lunch with their therapist. They see them interacting with their coworkers. They stop their therapist in the hallway to tell them about their recent blood-test results.

These settings influence therapy. For example, a therapist may receive regular updates about their client's behavior. They hear about the client lying to their case manager or breaking a specific rule. They listen to them complain about another client in session, only to observe them laughing with that same person an hour later. There are benefits and downsides to this information, but all of it impacts how we treat our clients

Private practice offers the highest form of client containment. Therapists typically meet with their clients once per week for about an hour. Distinct boundaries define the parameters regarding additional contact. Beyond emergencies or unplanned run-ins, most therapists don't see or hear from their clients outside of designated meeting times.

Of course, such minimal interaction can also impact treatment. The client may act one way in the office, but they are entirely different elsewhere. Without any additional information about the client's behavior, conceptualization can, at times, be quite challenging.

Obtaining Clients

In agencies, directors or supervisors typically assign clients to each therapist. Therapists may volunteer or request clients based on their caseloads, but they usually don't need to market themselves. Furthermore, typically speaking, the therapist doesn't earn less money that week if a client cancels or no-shows. Their paychecks are usually fixed by salary or hourly amounts—these wages aren't determined by the number of clients they see.

In private practice, therapists must obtain and secure their clients. This is the business part of therapy, and it can be hard! Therapists accepting insurance may receive a consistent stream of in-network referrals. But private-pay therapists network and market their services. Either way, therapists must spend the time or money (usually, it's a combination of both!) to attract new clients.

Mandated Clients

In agencies, many therapists have caseloads full of court-mandated or other types of mandated clients. Some of these clients exhibit motivation for growth and self-awareness. However, some of them just want to satisfy their treatment requirements and move on.

I've treated many of these clients, and our work together was vital in strengthening my therapeutic skills. Mandated work taught me so much about modern society—about the role of privilege in mental health, racism and discrimination, and the obvious cracks within our legal system. It also taught me about my *own* biases and advantages as a middle-class, white woman. As therapists, we must be willing to reflect on these parts of ourselves.

Earning Potential

Fewer topics enrage therapists more than salaries. Therapist pay varies on many factors: level of experience, geographical location, type of agency work, and negotiation skills. The spectrum is vast. Some agencies pay nothing at all, and others pay entry-level therapists close to six figures.

When understanding your total compensation, you must consider the monetary value of your company's employee benefits. Benefits, including your health insurance, paid time off, retirement savings plans and employer matches, flexible spending accounts (FSAs), and health savings accounts (HSAs), are often at least 30% of your compensation.

Many people assume private practitioners make a lot of money. This can be true, but it's a short-sighted assumption. While successful private-practice therapists usually earn more per hour than agency-based therapists, those fees do not account for all the expenses associated with owning a business. Office rent, furniture, marketing expenses, listing fees, liability insurance, supplies and materials, and health insurance add up!

Aim to BE FAIR in the Workplace

As a therapist, you already regularly think about how you impact your clients. If you work in an agency, you also must consider how you impact your supervisors and colleagues. I recommend you consider the "BE FAIR" acronym when navigating the workplace.

B: Brainstorm Solutions

E: Employee Awareness

F: Flexibile

A: Altruistic

I: Integrate Feedback

R: Reliable

B: Brainstorm Solutions

When people talk about valuing a team player, they mean they value someone who contributes thoughtful ideas and collaborates well with others. For this reason, I can't emphasize the importance of problem-solving skills enough. When you have problem-solving skills, you proactively consider how to address various issues. Even if the solutions aren't viable, an imperfect solution is better than no solution. Supervisors and colleagues appreciate forward-thinking, self-sufficient therapists. Do your best to make that happen.

Always think about how you can fix an issue before you start complaining about it. When a problem arises, consider what you need before you barge into your boss's office.

Expertise is irrelevant without problem-solving skills. It doesn't matter how skilled you are in a specific therapy model if you can't think critically. In the workplace, one person's helplessness affects everyone. If other people need to remedy your problem, that occupies their time and mental energy. Over time, they will resent you for your helplessness.

E: Employee Awareness

Working with others can be one of the best or worst parts of the job. We've all had annoying colleagues; we've all worked with people and wondered why they were ever hired.

But when you work for an organization, you must remember that you don't control how it operates. You have only your job. I don't condone accepting toxic work environments, but I encourage you to recognize that you won't agree with some workplace decisions. You won't always approve of how others do their jobs.

Employee awareness means respecting the company's chain of command. Report to the person you're supposed to report to. If you don't know who that is, ask. If your chain of command is broken (or makes no sense), these signs might indicate a toxic work environment, which I address in more detail later.

Regardless of your feelings, don't undermine others. It's demeaning, childish, and ineffective. Avoid making generalized assumptions about other people's work ethic. And don't criticize someone's work, especially if you don't understand the scope of their job fully.

F: Flexible

Flexible therapists adapt to change and pivot themselves to new expectations with minimal hesitation. In other words, you handle shit—even if you don't really feel like it.

Good therapists exercise flexibility with their clients. People come in with different needs, moods, and demands each day. Expect a degree of uncertainty with their behavior—life itself is so uncertain.

Finally, good employees also exercise flexibility in the workplace. Offer help when a group needs coverage. Take that new client who needs an intake. Don't lose complete control if the power goes out and erases the note you finally started writing.

A: Altruistic

Altruism means having concern for the welfare of others. Bosses value having collaborative teams, and excellent employees help their team with their knowledge, time, and kindness.

Altruism doesn't need to be complicated to be effective. Just focus on being friendly and inclusive, and take advantage of helping with small gestures. Start the pot of coffee when you arrive at work. Loan a book if you think a colleague could benefit from the material. Share your art supplies if someone needs them.

I: Integration of Feedback

A supervisor once told me she wanted me to share my thoughts more often in our staff meetings. Her request triggered the traumatic recall of sitting in a parent-teacher conference, where my teacher pointed at my report card and told my parents, "She's such a pleasure, but she's too shy!"

I lean toward shyness and introversion—it's who I am. I've spent years working through my socialization fears. Today, I can mostly fake an outgoing, extroverted persona if needed. So when my supervisor gave me this feedback, it jolted me back to being eight years old. I was back in that parent-teacher conference, gritting my teeth, averting my gaze, and sitting in a shadow of my own shame. I thanked my supervisor, told her I'd work on it, left her office, and cried.

There isn't an easy way to integrate feedback. If you're looking for a magic trick from me, I don't have one. I wanted to keep growing, so I had to keep pushing myself. I needed to talk more in meetings.

Remember that motivation is optional, but discipline is necessary. When your boss gives you feedback, it usually indicates they want you to do something about it now. Don't just smile and nod and disregard what they say. Don't make a half-assed attempt. And don't wait until you feel motivated to work on it. Instead, absorb the feedback and prioritize it—even if it's the last thing you want to do.

R: Reliable

Reliability is the glue that keeps every successful company running. People shop on Amazon for its reliable, two-day shipping. They buy the newest iPhone for the reliable Apple experience. They spend a week at Disneyland for a reliable family vacation.

When reliability is automatic, people rarely consider the competition. We don't need to think about other options if we've had consistently positive experiences. We only consider alternatives when we feel wronged, or when the company starts becoming unreliable.

Reliable employees keep everyone happy. No matter the industry, your reliability is invaluable. Strive to exude this trait everywhere you go. Be dependable. If you commit to a task, get it done.

Do Your Paperwork on Time and Avoid Making Excuses

As therapists, we've all complained and commiserated about keeping notes. Sometimes we procrastinate and fall behind. But late paperwork doesn't just affect your supervisor or your mental well-being. It can also be a severe liability.

While working in a residential treatment facility, I treated a young woman struggling with alcohol use disorder. She also had mild depression and post-traumatic stress disorder. We spent our mid-morning session processing the building tension she felt toward her mother.

That day, she presented as guarded and withdrawn. This demeanor wasn't abnormal—she typically presented this way. Our session ended with us discussing the new boundary she intended to set with her mother. She told me that she was looking forward to having a movie night with her friends that evening.

The rest of my afternoon was busy. I met with my other clients, and I felt especially tired by the end of the day. I left the office and told myself I would finish my paperwork the next morning.

A few hours later, my supervisor called me. She told me my client had just barely survived a suicide attempt and was now recovering in the hospital.

I didn't respond for a moment. The shock passed through me, penetrating my consciousness. I shared my surprise with my supervisor. She said she understood and attempted to comfort me. "Are you okay?" she asked. "Do you need anything from me? How are you planning to take care of yourself tonight?"

I don't remember my answers, but I do remember how quickly she transitioned into more formal questioning: "When did you last meet with her? Did you assess for suicidal ideation? You saw her today? Where is her note? I'm not seeing anything in the system."

At her last question, I paused and took in a sharp breath. I didn't have a good answer—nothing made sense. I waited for her to fire me. And because I tend to catastrophize and imagine worst-case scenarios, I anticipated a lawsuit and losing my ability to practice.

What clues had I missed? Was I completely inept? Would this have happened had she been working with a better therapist?

The perils of this clinical situation haunted me for weeks. I dreamt about my client—I couldn't focus on anything else. What if she had died? Losing a client to suicide shatters the therapist's soul. It stabs and twists into every crevice of our competence. Nothing scares us more.

I worried about the legal ramifications. What if someone requested my documentation? What if my client had told her friends or parents or doctor that she had met with me that day? What if she had told them she couldn't understand why I didn't see how much she was struggling? Why hadn't I just written that damn note?

My client was okay. She survived. Life went on for both of us. But I've never procrastinated on doing my notes again. We are not mind-readers. People commit suicide without talking about it. We can't account for every potential outcome. We can only do our best. But doing our best means completing our paperwork. On time, and preferably as soon as possible.

Do Not Avoid Crisis Situations

To extrapolate from my last story, I want to discuss the sensitive nature of crisis situations. They happen. A client will feel suicidal. Another client will disclose child or elder abuse. These moments feel very scary, especially when you're inexperienced.

Unfortunately, many therapists skirt around potential crisis issues. Often, this skirting is unintentional. They worry about saying the wrong thing. For instance, they believe that asking a direct question about suicide might plant the idea in someone's head. They recognize when they're heading toward potential speculation, and they might divert from the topic altogether. They don't talk about these diversion tactics to their supervisors or colleagues. But they do it, and they do it because they feel anxious.

Of course, this strategy is unsustainable. On a conceptual level, if you avoid talking about delicate details, what does this discomfort demonstrate to your clients? What does it say about your willingness to discuss their vulnerability and taboo truths?

Furthermore, on a logistical level, therapists agree to fulfill our mandated reporting responsibilities. You commit to routinely screen, assess, and treat clients struggling with life-threatening situations. Therefore, the failure to act is negligent.

I believe most therapists understand the importance of tackling difficult issues head-on. But many therapists avoid direct questioning. They don't want to seem abrasive or presumptuous. And let's be honest: nobody *likes* making a mandated report. It's uncomfortable, and it can be damaging to our clients and our relationships with them.

First, acknowledge that mandated reporting isn't about feeling comfortable. It's about abiding by our duties. If you have even a slight inkling of an assumption of danger, you must *go there*.

In my experience, my supervisors readily helped me when it came to managing crisis issues. After all, I was working under their licenses. They couldn't risk me jeopardizing their liability. Additionally, they understood the fear and uncertainty associated with managing these situations. They know that it's distressing. They know that you feel inexperienced.

I'lladmitthatIstrugglewiththeethicalcomponents associated with mandated reporting. I know that hospitalizations can cause retraumatization. I realize child abuse reports often result in even more punitive punishment. Finally, I understand that breaching confidentiality, even when required and even when we tirelessly debrief our clients about it, may forever alter the alliance we share.

But for now, this is the system we have, and this is the system we need to work within.

Track Your Work Achievements

I've spent time talking about the importance of advocating for your monetary worth. We can and should advocate for more money, prestige, and responsibility. We're on the frontlines of the human soul—we deal with the inner mechanics of emotions, trauma, and social relationships. Our work is incredibly important.

Yet we cringe and cower when it comes time to discuss compensation. We still rationalize insulting salaries. As discussed earlier, we tell ourselves we're "paying our dues." We convince ourselves we don't care about money.

And that can be true. We all want to make a meaningful difference in this world. And that's fantastic and virtuous, but we still have bills to pay, food to eat, and new clothes to buy.

Unfortunately, many employees lose themselves in the daily cog of billable hours and endless meetings. Then, the time comes when you want a pay raise or feel ready for a new job. But once it's time to overhaul your cover letter and resume, you don't know how to display your accomplishments.

This is why I recommend tracking your work achievements. What assets have you brought to your company? Did you start a new support group or lead a killer presentation? Did you receive specialized training? Did you change the intake questionnaire to include more culturally sensitive screening inquiries? Write it down! Write it down right after you achieve it. If you wait, you'll forget.

Your massive list of awesomeness isn't to share with anyone else. You're just keeping your accomplishments fresh—tucking them into your pocket for whenever you need the reminder.

Be Vulnerable During Every Group Supervision

I want to be in the arena. I want to be brave with my life. And when we make the choice to dare greatly, we sign up to get our asses kicked. We can choose courage or we can choose comfort, but we can't have both. Not at the same time. Vulnerability is not about winning or losing; it's having the courage to show up and be seen when we have no control over the outcome. Vulnerability is not weakness; it's our greatest measure of courage. A lot of cheap seats in the area are filled with people who never venture onto the floor. They just hurt mean-spirited criticisms and put-downs from a safe distance. The problem is, when we stop caring what people think and stop feeling hurt by cruelty, we lose our ability to connect. But when we're defined by what people think, we lose the courage to be vulnerable. Therefore, we need to be selective about the feedback we let into our lives. For me, if you're not in the area getting your ass kicked, I'm not interested in your feedback. — Brené Brown, Rising Strong

I once worked with a colleague who loved sharing about her brilliant therapeutic moments. In every group supervision, she presented another miraculous epiphany. One client no longer exhibited any anxiety symptoms! The next client reconciled twenty years of estrangement with his brother, after just one session! She convinced another client to become a therapist.

She was a good therapist, but I believed she used supervision to embellish and brag about her achievements. At times, I felt so frustrated when she talked.

Our growth doesn't emerge from the good sessions. Our growth comes from the willingness to identify our mistakes—it comes from the courage to reflect on the ugly, painful moments that we want to pretend never happened.

I know that it's painful to feel inferior. We don't want our professors or supervisors or colleagues to judge us for our vulnerabilities. So we hold back. We attempt to protect our reputation. Conversely, we lose the benefit of supervision. We miss the opportunity for growth and reflection.

At the same time, we expect our clients to delve into their feelings with us. I'm no stranger to this discrepancy. As much as I welcome vulnerability in my clients, I struggle with it myself. The dissonance is real—the hypocrisy has always tormented me.

And yet, group supervision is a common, and often helpful, part of our clinical arena. It's where we can expose ourselves, where we can choose to share the ugly parts of our work and our insecurities. So speak up. Share your failures. Ask the question that you keep avoiding asking. Speak when it's painful.

Do you still feel scared? I get it. Talk about it in your own therapy. Meditate over it. Journal your fears. But, at some point, in some capacity, if you really want the growth, if you really want to strengthen your skills and progress in your career, you'll need to enter the arena.

Learn How to Cope With A Problematic Supervisor

Many barriers can inevitably impede the supervision relationship. Some supervisors are so overworked that they struggle to find the time to meet with you for a single hour each week. When they can squeeze in an appointment, you must compete with constant interruptions—phone calls, email alerts, knocks on the door, the lunch they've been trying to eat for the past three hours. Often, this isn't their fault. They're pawns of an inefficient system.

Other supervisors don't know the difference between being a therapist and being a supervisor. They validate your struggles, but they dig into your personal problems instead of helping you help your clients. Rather than helping you to improve your therapy skills, they try to improve your life.

Finally, just like some therapists shouldn't be therapists, some supervisors just shouldn't be supervisors. Usually, if this is the case, your frustrations aren't unique. Others often question how that person landed this job, too. Maybe they are a friend of the CEO's daughter's pet hamster. Maybe it was a matter of dumb luck. Or maybe the company couldn't pay for anyone better. I'll discuss some solutions if that's the case.

Talk to Your Supervisor About Your Concerns

Some supervisors might seem completely inept, but others are surprisingly receptive to feedback. Most supervisors want to support the therapists they work with. They want to see them grow and succeed. Just like we value our clients giving us feedback, most supervisors value it as well.

If you intend to speak to your supervisor about any concerns, I recommend you identify your desired outcomes. Be as specific and concrete as possible. It's not helpful to say, "I don't think I'm getting what I need from supervision." This is vague, and it can come across as helpless. Instead, identify what you need. Do you want more help with interventions? More support in understanding your countertransference? Guidance in strengthening your boundaries with clients?

Talk To Their Supervisor (If That Option Exists)

In some cases, you may need to talk to your supervisor's supervisor. This may apply if your supervisor is breaking the law or acting unethically with clients or supervisees. It can also apply if you've already spoken to your supervisor, and they continue to dismiss your needs.

However, you shouldn't barge into the CEO's office insisting that your supervisor harassed another therapist. Instead, take a moment, collect the facts, and write them down. Express your concern openly, but aim to present the facts with objectivity.

Lean on Your Colleagues

Collaborating with other therapists can rectify some of the stress associated with a dreadful supervisor. I'm not suggesting that this is an equivalent strategy to having a competent mentor. But strong relationships with colleagues can offer other professional perspectives and feedback. Moreover, it helps you strengthen your network, which may help you leave your job faster, if that's what you choose to do!

Determine If You Can Seek Outside Supervision

If you are experiencing problems with your current supervisor, you can see if you can work with someone else outside the organization. Some places will allow you to do this, and others might have reasons why you can't. You will probably have to pay for outside supervision. Make sure you get what you pay for! I recommend gathering a few quotes in your area to determine the appropriate market rates. Select a supervisor like you would vet any professional. Choose someone who:

- helps you grow into your theory.
- challenges you to evolve as a person.
- professionally explores countertransference.
- leaves you thinking and reflecting about yourself and your clients.

Stop Procrastinating Submitting Your Accrued Hours for Licensing Eligibility

I consider myself a writer, but I've always dreamed of being an author. I've had my name in print—in blog articles, editorial pieces, and many other published materials. But I have never published a book, and I've had this goal since I was seven. Most writers and aspiring writers consider publishing a book as the ultimate pinnacle: it's the Eagle Scout rank, the 26.2-mile marathon, the trek up Mount Everest.

Yet publishing a book is as exhausting as it is terrifying. Will my rambling thoughts make sense to anyone else? Do therapists really care what I have to say? What if I've devoted all this time to writing, editing, and preparing this manuscript, and everyone hates it?

I've procrastinated writing certain sections. I've surrendered to the temptations of emails and snacks and annoying my dog and texting my friends. As a working new mother, I also have time constraints. All of these excuses are valid. I could continue making these excuses for the rest of my life. But procrastination isn't about time management or distractions or laziness. Procrastination is always about fear.

If you struggle with perfectionism, you might fear putting in the work when you can't guarantee the outcome. I know is the case for me. I also fear I'm a fraud, so I procrastinate to avoid manifesting that fear. Instead of committing to trudging through— despite that fear—it feels safer to remain exactly where we are. Other times, procrastination is more about feeling overwhelmed by the sequence of events or the energy required to engage in the task.

I know many intelligent therapists who waited years before getting licensed. They had completed their hours and accrued enough experience. But they procrastinated about submitting their paperwork and taking their board exams.

First, I want to dismantle any notion that having a title or passing a test proves your therapeutic abilities. They don't. They're just quantitative measurements, and they reveal nothing about your effectiveness with clients. But you need those titles. And you need to pass those tests.

You've come this far. You completed school, and you slogged through all those clinical hours. That's a huge commitment, and it's an impressive achievement. But when we run marathons, we don't stop running at the twenty-fifth mile. When we write books, we don't edit all the chapters except for the last one. We persist. Finish what you started. You deserve it.

CHAPTER 7:

HOW TO ACTUALLY SET BOUNDARIES WHEN YOU SUCK AT SETTING BOUNDARIES

The difference between successful people and really successful people is that really successful people say no to almost everything. —Warren Buffet

The Therapist's Master Checklist of Poor Boundaries

- Engaging in sexual relations with clients

- Acting defensively when given negative feedback

- Tiptoeing around sensitive issues with clients

- Accepting late payment

- Overly self-disclosing

- Saying very little in session

- Pushing specific therapeutic interventions onto clients

- Giving too much direct advice

- Communicating with clients like they are friends

- Trying to convince clients they need to work on particular issues

- Seeking constant reassurance from clients or colleagues

- Failing to address no-shows

- Permitting sessions to regularly start or end later than they should

- Imposing personal moral beliefs onto clients

- Communicating unnecessarily or excessively with clients between sessions

- Fostering a sense of therapist dependency with clients

- Enabling client dependency

- Taking on the obligations of other colleagues

- Continuing to remain in toxic working conditions

- Avoiding making changes when feeling overworked

- Lacking an after-hours protocol

Why Are Therapeutic Boundaries So Hard?

Boundaries terrify many therapists; the struggles we experience with clients can closely mimic other interpersonal conflicts in our lives. A therapist who lingers at parties because she doesn't want to leave first may struggle with ending sessions on time. Another therapist who avoids telling his father that his insensitive comments hurt him might avoid confronting clients when they exhibit concerning behavior.

The need for setting boundaries triggers countertransference, and countertransference triggers the need for setting boundaries. I once worked with a client who often called me in between our sessions. At the time, I requested that clients contact me only in the event of emergencies. But this client had shared an extensive history of neglect. Her mother died when she was young; her father quickly remarried and spent most of my client's childhood doting on his new wife and her son. In her early twenties, she came home and found her new husband in the shower with another man.

Betrayed and heartbroken, she refused to date for many years. Until she changed her mind. The first time she called me, she wanted to update me on how much she had enjoyed dinner with her coworker. She hadn't expected much beyond a free meal, but he had been polite and charming. Our phone conversation was short. I told her I was so happy that she had a good time, and that I looked forward to talking about it more in our next session.

Then she called a few days later to tell me about a fight she had with her father. For a few weeks, I justified my decision to answer her calls. I knew her history, and I didn't want to let her down like so many other people had. She needed a consistent figure who could attune to her needs—unconditionally. I wanted to be that person.

And then my phone died one night at the gym. When I came home and charged it, I had two voicemails and three text messages. She really needed to talk, she insisted. When I called her back, she told me that she wasn't sure which insurance plan to enroll in at work. She didn't want to make the wrong decision—could I help?

I had lost myself in my countertransference. In my attempt to embody a perfect mother figure, I had overstepped my objectivity and professionalism. None of this was her fault. Before we began working together, I had made it clear that I wanted her to contact me only in an emergency. But I had never reinforced this rule. She had no reason to think anything was wrong.

Most of us became therapists because we excel in empathy and compassion. When I first entered this field, I thought therapy meant listening, validating, and supporting whatever my clients needed. I didn't realize I also needed to be a healthy role model!

After all, when we think about a stereotypical therapist, what do we imagine? Someone who is patient, warm, and gracious—someone who listens without judgment, who wants to do everything they can to make their clients feel safe? Or someone who confronts a client for canceling their sessions three times in a row?

And yet, the best therapists can balance both roles. They can listen and offer support, while upholding boundaries to keep clients protected and secure.

Boundaries are hard because they vary from client to client. There are rarely any absolutes. Is it okay to hug a client? If so, when and whom? When can we defer taking a payment because we know they will bring money next week? If we say we respond only to emergency phone calls, is there ever room for making an exception?

Although we may want to maintain universal boundaries, our clients come to us with different levels of insight and types of transference. They impact us in all sorts of ways. They pull emotions out of us, and those emotions can be intense and confusing. Our boundaries sometimes look different with different clients. We aren't going to set boundaries perfectly. It takes time, experience, and conscious practice to improve this skill. Therapists will fumble around and make mistakes. But through these errors, we will learn.

Why Boundaries Might Scare Therapists

When you think about it, unhealthy relationships are easy. We can act like rambunctious toddlers and yell or withdraw or fight as loudly as we want. We can ignore the other person's feelings and trample over their needs to focus on our own. We can break things and disregard rules and then ghost them altogether. We let our emotions dictate our actions, and we don't have to practice self-control. Then we can avoid personal responsibility when the relationship deteriorates.

Healthy relationships require much more work. We have to consider someone else's needs when we act. We must practice active listening, and we also need to convey our desires calmly and maturely. Being healthy takes work!

Often, our clients come to us after a series of disappointing relationships have failed them. They are reeling from the trauma from someone who hurt them. They feel distressed over their marriage. They can't say no to their parents. They don't know how to discipline their children. They attract the wrong friends.

Our clients depend on us to hold their relationship pains. But they often act out their relationship patterns with us in the same way they do with other people. This acting out is unconscious, but if we don't address it, we enable the pattern.

Boundaries might scare therapists because we often associate setting boundaries with setting cruel and rigid limits. Of course, we don't want to be mean. We don't want to hurt our clients in the ways so many other people have hurt them. We worry our boundaries will push them away, that they will deem us as harsh and invalidating.

Many of us entered this field because we wanted to be perfect listeners who healed our clients. We didn't consider the logistics of being a working professional. But these logistics are essential. They separate our careers from friendships, romantic relationships, and any other professional dynamic in our clients' lives. We owe it to our clients to remain safe and consistent with them. It is our job to set and uphold the boundaries, no matter how the client presents. We need to do what they cannot do for themselves. Although we want to be warm and compassionate healers, true healing sometimes comes from setting boundaries and even upsetting our clients.

Identifying When You Need to Set a Boundary

My husband is phenomenal at setting boundaries. He honors his integrity, and he doesn't let people take advantage of him. When he expresses his needs, he is calm, level-headed, and assertive. Most importantly, people know what they can expect from him. Despite his audience or mood, he remains consistent in how he speaks and acts.

I admire how he makes boundaries look easy.

I have spent thousands of dollars paying therapists to teach me about boundaries, a problem I've always struggled with. I tend to be passive, but I can also be passive-aggressive, and I tend to care about other people's needs before my own. If someone hurts my feelings, I often withhold telling them, unless we're very close. So, in writing this section, I consulted with my husband. Our first conversation went something like this:

Me: Babe, when should people set boundaries?

Husband: (doesn't look up from his cell phone game) When they feel disrespected, uncomfortable, or underappreciated.

Me: Of course. But what else?

Husband: That's it.

Me: But I need to make this section in the book longer.

Husband: But that's it.

How supremely unhelpful, right? Of course, people should set boundaries when they feel disrespected, uncomfortable, or underappreciated. That's obvious!

But, he's right—that's it! What else is there to say? That's the frustrating part about boundaries. They are shockingly straightforward. If someone hurts us, tell them. If a relationship isn't working, do something about it. It's obvious, isn't it? It would be if we didn't have our emotions.

Baby Steps for Setting Boundaries

My husband is an intelligent man, and he's an incredible therapist. We need to follow his direction and set boundaries when we feel disrespected, uncomfortable, and underappreciated. But how do we achieve such a colossal task?

Enter the ultimate baby steps.

Step 1: Reflect on Your Relationship with Boundaries

Why do we say yes when we mean no? Why do we enable people to keep hurting us? Why do we avoid saying something when something must be said? Boundaries are difficult for most people, and therapists aren't exempt from the struggle. Like with everything we do in our work, the growth starts by enhancing internal awareness.

I. What messages did you receive about boundaries in your family of origin?

Our families are our first templates for boundaries, and their modeling impacts us for the rest of our lives. How did your caregivers set limits for you? Did the limits feel fair? Were they consistent with their expectations? And what happened when someone crossed a boundary? How did family members communicate their needs to one another? Were children encouraged to share their opinions? Common examples of boundary issues in family systems include:

- Abuse (physical, emotional, sexual, financial).

- Neglect of basic physical or emotional needs.

- Parents depending on their children for emotional support.

- Lack of physical or emotional privacy.

- Parents unable or unwilling to act as a united front for children.

- One parent holding all the authority in the household.

- Inconsistent or complete lack of rules.

- Nonexistent or overly excessive discipline when breaking defined rules.

II. How do you feel when someone sets a boundary with you?

You know that boundaries are important, but how does it feel to be on the receiving end? What reactions do you have toward the other person? Respect? Admiration? Relief that someone else set the guidelines? And how do you feel when a boundary offends you?

III. When have you set a boundary before? What made you act differently that time?

It's often beneficial for us to examine exceptions to fixed rules. In the past, when have you expressed and implemented a boundary? Do you find it easier to set boundaries with close loved ones or strangers? Are there any differences in how you set limits in your personal life compared to your professional life?

Step 2: Assume People Are Good

I believe most people are good people, and I hope you agree. Isn't that why we're therapists? Because we assume that people are inherently worthy? Because we know that people—despite their flaws and mistakes—can change and grow and make the world a better place? If we can't believe people are good, who can?

I operate under the notion that people move through their days trying to meet their own needs. For the most part, they're doing the best they can in a given moment. At times, I don't agree with someone's decisions or thought processes. Of course I wish I could change certain things. But I don't believe most people walk around this planet conjuring a convoluted plot to destroy my life. Instead, I believe they're focused on themselves, just like I'm mostly focused on myself.

Many times, we think of boundaries as an exclusive "me problem." *I've been hurt. I've been violated. I've been taken advantage of in some way.*

We are always entitled to our feelings. We can feel betrayed, upset, violated, disrespected, and otherwise hurt by people. These are real experiences, and we can and should honor them. But caring about only our side of the story can limit the story itself. We can discuss limits without trying to alienate others. Relationships are the beating heart driving human behavior. If we believe that people are inherently good, we react less intensely to distress. We assume that people generally don't want to hurt us—we trust that the world is relatively safe.

Assuming people are good isn't a specific action. It's a mindset, and this mindset sets the framework for boundaries. Honoring the goodness comes down to choosing to believe three basic narratives:

- **Most people value and crave connection.**

- **Most people don't want to hurt other people.**

- **Most people feel afraid, sad, guilty, or ashamed if they hurt someone they care about.**

When we believe these narratives, we can navigate interpersonal issues more efficiently. We tend to be more conscious of everyone's needs, which makes us better people. We live and honor the goodness of other people. As a result, setting boundaries feels less scary. We can discuss limits without trying to alienate others.

Of course, there are exceptions to this rule, and they include instances of abuse, direct threats or hostility, or any other time we feel physically or emotionally unsafe. In those cases, our safety trumps everything else, and we don't owe anyone a reason for setting limits.

Step 3: Own Personal Responsibility

As I mentioned, many people struggle with boundaries because we don't want to hurt other people. Additionally, we may have tried setting limits in the past, but we didn't like the outcome. Maybe the other person acted defensively. Perhaps they convinced us to change our minds and return to our status quo.

When setting boundaries, we often focus on the other person's wrongful behavior. Our boundaries act as weapons demanding what we need other people to do differently. Even if we package the boundary nicely, the other person often reacts with anger or sadness. They still feel attacked.

You can start setting effective boundaries by acknowledging the part you play in a specific dynamic. Owning personal responsibility demonstrates maturity. My husband, the boundary king, has taught me this critical life lesson. When we argue, he almost immediately acknowledges what he did wrong. Because he does this, I then feel more inclined to reflect and acknowledge my part in the conflict. Instead of attacking each other by saying awful insults we will later regret, both of us look inward to focus on how we can each change and grow.

Step 4: Disregard I-Statements and Find Your Arc

If you're looking for the section on I-statements, you won't find it in my book. I-statements are a specific style of communication that focus on the speaker's thoughts or feelings. Most I-statements follow the format, "I feel _____ when you ____."

I'm not keen on I-statements. I find that they seem incomplete, and they often trigger the other person's guilt. And when people feel guilty, they become defensive. Therefore, even if my I-statement technically sets my boundary, it never feels like I've reached much resolution. Instead, I use the ARC strategy, which I find to be far more beneficial.

A: Acknowledge your part: Identify the role you play in the dynamic.

R: Report the issue: State exactly what's bothering you.

C: Collaborate on a solution: Invite the other person to help you improve the situation.

Vignette #1: My client persistently arrives late for her session a few minutes late. She offers a different excuse for her tardiness each week. After four sessions, I address the issue.

Acknowledge your part: *I want to acknowledge that I made a mistake by waiting this long to say something.*

Report the issue: *I've noticed our sessions have started late over the past month.*

Collaborate on a solution: *I know you have a lot going on, but it's so important to me that we get our full time together. How can I best support you in making that happen?*

Reflection: I recognized that I had failed to set and implement an appropriate therapeutic boundary. Instead, I allowed my client to continue arriving late without addressing it. To attempt to resolve the issue, I chose to start by highlighting my mistake. I wanted to give her the benefit of the doubt and emphasize the importance of our work. I asked her how we could collaborate to achieve that.

Vignette #2: My client enters the session and immediately compliments my dress and says that I look really pretty. He then comments that my boyfriend is fortunate to be dating me. I thank the client, continue the session, but find myself becoming increasingly anxious and unsettled.

Acknowledge your part: *I want to acknowledge that I have found myself withdrawing from you.*

Report the issue: *When I reflect on it, I realize I began feeling this way when you complimented my dress.*

Collaborate on a solution: *I know you are a warm and caring person. While I appreciate the gesture of* *you acknowledging me, it's important that I emphasize the nature of our professional relationship. That being said, I wonder if we can talk more about our dynamic. I think it could be helpful to discuss your feelings about therapy and clarify our boundaries.*

Reflection: I started the conversation by acknowledging how I reacted to his compliment. I was direct in identifying my part. I focused on validating his strengths and intentions, but I also highlighted the need for reviewing boundaries and discussing his comment within the context of our therapy.

Step 5: When in Doubt, Praise and Validate

Everyone loves praise and validation. *Everyone.* Even when they pretend they don't. That's why I believe in wrapping boundaries with kindness.

Kindness isn't disingenuous. If we believe people are inherently good, it's easy to tap into identifying their strengths. Some simple examples of praise and validation include:

- I'm really impressed by how you...
- I'm so glad you...
- I am happy you...
- That was so brave of you.
- Thank you for sharing that with me.
- You're really improving in...
- You're making such progress by...

- I know that must have been so hard.

- I can't imagine how scary that must have felt.

- You are doing such a great job.

- I am so proud of you.

Step 6: Anticipate Pushback

One time, a client didn't pay me for two sessions in a row. I had never worked with someone who didn't pay on time. After the first time, I dismissed it. She left her wallet at home. Everyone is forgetful sometimes, I reasoned.

The second time, she had rent due and her car broke down on the same day. She promised to have the money by the following week. I could feel myself becoming angry and resentful, but I didn't tell her. I knew she wasn't trying to cause problems. But I felt frustrated at myself for acting passively. In our third session, just after she began talking about how she had loaned her sister money, I knew I needed to set the boundary.

Acknowledge your part: *When I heard you talk about loaning your sister money, I noticed myself feeling a bit on edge.*

Report the issue: *It made me realize that I have neglected to talk about the importance of payment during our last few sessions.*

Collaborate on a solution: *I know you have a lot going on, and I know that you also value our therapy. I am hoping we can discuss finding a solution for* *making consistent payments each week. What's the best method for making sure this happens?*

She exploded. "Are we really going to be talking about money right now? I'm dealing with an emergency. Do you even care?"

I felt ashamed immediately. This dynamic would be tough for most therapists. We want to keep our clients happy, but happiness isn't always the goal of therapy. She felt attacked by my boundary. At that moment, I reminded her of all the other people who had taken advantage of her. Fortunately, we could talk about this pattern in her life.

I responded, "I completely understand you feeling overwhelmed right now. I know you are going through a lot. I imagine it's stressful to come to session needing support, and your therapist makes a comment about needing payment. I would probably be frustrated, too."

Then, I waited for her response. I want to emphasize that I didn't feel brave or brilliant in that moment. I felt fairly confident she'd stand up and leave. Instead, she laughed and apologized for her reaction. By validating her feelings and acknowledging my role in the dynamic, I left space for her to assume responsibility for her actions. Furthermore, I tolerated the distress associated with her pushback. Instead of acting defensively, I validated her and offered her the opportunity to reflect on her feelings as well. This allowed us both to move forward in finding a realistic solution and deepening our therapeutic relationship.

Still, I don't want to make myself sound like a therapy genius. This moment was incredibly uncomfortable, and I spent the rest of my day doubting myself. Had I been too harsh? How should I have worded my needs differently? Why hadn't I said anything the previous week? Or the week before that? And would she come back to therapy? Did she still question if I cared about her?

At times, we'll do everything right and we'll still encounter pushback. Setting boundaries can be uncomfortable. Likewise, they require ongoing consistency to be effective. We can't just tell people what we need from them once and expect automatic change. If it were that easy, we wouldn't fear boundaries in the first place.

Prepare for this discomfort. When you feel it, I encourage you to acknowledge and even celebrate your willingness to embark on this journey. The discomfort symbolizes your growth; it indicates you're making a change.

Step 7: Continue Reminding Yourself of the Benefits

We will all encounter people who don't respect or understand our boundaries. When this happens, it's normal to experience doubt, guilt, or shame. When I struggle with boundaries, I continue to remind myself of the benefits, including:

- healthier relationships.

- honoring my personal integrity.

- healthy modeling for our clients.

- realistic expectations of the therapy process.

When we teach our clients boundaries, they can share and practice what they have learned with other people. And that creates a prosocial, ripple effect throughout our society.

The benefits of boundaries outweigh the risks, but these benefits may not always be apparent in the short-term. After all, setting boundaries can lead to relationship ruptures. Those ruptures require attentiveness and compassion. That said, people who truly respect you will respect the limits you set. If they can't even do that, it's time to reassess that relationship.

CHAPTER 8:

HOW TO COPE WITH BURNOUT AND FATIGUE BEFORE YOU HATE YOUR LIFE

I frequently receive messages and questions related to these topics. New and experienced clinicians alike feel uncertain about burnout. They wonder if their feelings are normal. They worry that they can't help themselves—or their clients. Let's talk about it.

Don't Assume You Are Immune to Burnout

One day, during my graduate school traineeship, I sat in group supervision. It was summertime and warm outside. Earlier that morning, I had gone to the beach to enjoy the sunshine. I'd even brought a therapy book to read. I was so young and so eager to be the best therapist.

I loved supervision. I loved soaking in everything I could learn about this field. I sat at the round table with my iced coffee and spiral notebook plastered with clichéd quotes about *something, something, life is a journey.* I was ready to jot down my super important notes, ready for my supervisor to nourish me with her knowledge and insight.

My supervisor began by checking in with each of us about our week. One of my colleagues expressed how utterly exhausted he felt. He shared his hesitation about this career and diverted for a moment to muse about alternative paths in business or real estate. His honest admission intrigued my supervisor. She then asked all of us to discuss our experiences with burnout.

I had nothing to contribute. I pitied my colleague. That's right. Pity! I also felt confused by his statements. How could he feel so exhausted? How could he feel anything but super jazzed and passionate about helping others?

I now reflect on my naive moment often. My colleague foreshadowed the same exhaustion I would feel just a few years later. Because no matter how much we love the work, sitting and untangling other people's emotional baggage does become exhausting. Our passion, no matter how fiery it starts out, can wane over time. The reality of this field rarely matches our expectations. Clients test us, agencies push our limits, and we also have to balance the delicacy of our work with our personal lives.

I want to make it clear that we can be amazing therapists and still question the career. Burnout is real. We will all experience it to some degree. It's simply a matter of noticing when it happens and how we react to it.

Burnout Happens Very, Very Slowly

Have you ever fallen in love? The kind of dizzying love where the world feels complete and the concept of happily-ever-after doesn't seem so far-fetched? The kind where the sex shatters you and your lover's long-winded text messages melt your cold and pessimistic heart?

The honeymoon phase of falling in love is spellbinding. We're delusional—almost as detached from reality as young children are when they play make-believe. The honeymoon phase doesn't just disappear one day. It slowly evaporates—and you don't even recognize when it's happening. Instead, you start noticing when your partner leaves wrappers on the counters. You feel agitated at how loudly they talk on the phone. You can't understand why they never unload the dishwasher or pick the right cheese at the grocery store.

Maybe the date nights become more predictable, the sex slows down, and the compliments wane. Maybe you two start arguing more. The novelty and excitement dissipate. At times, you might even wonder if this is the right relationship for you.

Many therapists assume burnout is this grand event. But it's not. Burnout is a gradual process that can unravel in prolonged phases. Like relationships, we rarely recognize what's happening until we reflect on how we once felt. Then we start reasoning with ourselves. We're just tired. That client is just particularly difficult. We need a vacation—that will recharge us. Some of these strategies work, at least in the short-term.

But eventually, we start wondering, *Whom or what I am defending here? Myself? My clients? My work altogether? Why am I so tired? Why are things so difficult?*

We become stagnant or complacent. We lose the initial sparks that drew us to the field. And because we assumed we were immune, we feel unequipped to deal with it once it's in front of us.

Whatever Led You to This Field Is Often the Contributing Factor to Your Burnout

Before I became a therapist, I idolized therapists. I thought they inspired and healed people for a living. They saved those who couldn't save themselves. I wanted to be that person. I wanted to listen, support, and rescue people.

Let's break down my thought process further. Like many therapists, I grew up as a quintessential listener. People confided in me with their secrets. From a young age, I received validation because of how safe others felt with me.

Also, like many therapists, I have struggled with low self-esteem. When my low self-esteem peaked in adolescence, my ability to deflect my problems by listening to others benefited me. I had many friends, and I fit in well with most people. I liked being needed. If I could help others, I reasoned, it meant I wasn't all that bad.

When I first started working as a therapist, I loved working with motivated, desperate clients. I almost reveled in their helplessness and felt important when they clung to me. I lacked confidence, and I internalized their clinginess as a sign I was doing a good job. Those clients could eradicate my painful feelings of incompetence. *Look how well I'm doing! Look at how important I am! They need me! I'm so special!*

I expected that feeling special would translate into having a happier and fuller life. But my reality was different. While I did feel like my work mattered, that belief didn't correspond to a more thriving life.

Saving others ultimately became tiring. What had changed? I no longer loved working with those motivated, desperate clients. Where the helplessness once thrilled me, I now felt exhausted by the attention they required. The clinginess became aggravating. Why did they need me so much? Why couldn't they respect my therapeutic boundaries? What made me so important, anyway?

I gravitated toward my aloof clients. When I went on vacation, they didn't mind my absence. I wasn't their rescuer, and it felt freeing. With them, I permitted myself to be detached. But once I discovered this shift—once I recognized that I wanted more detachment and less involvement, I realized I was burnt out.

Often, when we think about growth, we consider only what we gain. We don't think about what we lose. As I gained confidence in my therapy skills, I lost the need to feel so important and influential. By gaining satisfying relationships and exploring passions outside of work, I lost the desire for my job to be the most important part of my life.

Many therapists love the idea of healing, but we don't realize what healing takes from the healer. Healing takes our patience, countertransference, compassion, boredom, mistakes, and helplessness. At times, it can also take our identity.

The Anatomy of the Toxic Work Environment

Earlier, I discussed some of the obstacles associated with the workplace. Toxic work environments are one of the leading causes of therapist burnout. But it's challenging to discern what this toxicity actually means. Sometimes, the dysfunction is blatantly apparent. A supervisor having an affair with a supervisee. A therapist documenting notes for a session they didn't render. But most toxicity at the workplace exists within murky shades of gray—sometimes, we can rely only on that visceral feeling that things just aren't right. With that in mind, I've narrowed down some red flags to consider in assessing burnout factors at your job:

- Employees continually working outside of their scope of practice

- Ongoing workplace cattiness and gossip with no change or resolution

- Employees showing blatant disregard for client boundaries

- Working in physically unsafe conditions

- Employees breaking the law

- Extreme power differential between employees and management

- Chronically unrealistic work demands

- Lack of faith or respect for the company's mission

I've worked in a few toxic environments. I know what it feels like dealing with unprofessional management or unfit bosses, or abusive, unethical conditions. In my experience, walking away was the only resolution. But I won't pretend I came to that decision easily. Instead, I cycled through emotional whirlwinds and experienced all the stages of grief.

Shock:

- How is this company getting away with this?

- This can't really be happening.

- Mental health organizations wouldn't behave this way.

- How could I have missed that this was happening?

Denial

- It's probably not that bad.

- All companies make mistakes.

- All companies need to focus on making money.

- These same problems exist everywhere.

- Maybe these problems are just temporary.

Anger

- How dare they treat us this way?

- I'm so frustrated that my clients are getting caught in the crossfire.

- I'm furious that we're expected to give so much.

- I can't believe they're asking me to do this (unethical) thing.

- I hate my supervisor (or other members of upper management).

Sadness

- I feel sorry for my clients.

- I feel sorry for my boss (or other employees).

- I am sad that this organization isn't what I thought it was.

- I am sad that my clients are not receiving the care they deserve.

- I feel upset that I can't be the kind of therapist I want to be while I work here.

Bargaining (often the driving force that keeps us in a toxic environment)

- As long as I provide good therapy, I shouldn't worry about what the company is doing.

- I'll just stay at this company until I complete my hours/pay off my debt/become licensed/build my private practice.

- I need a job, and I can't leave this one until I have another one.

- As long as I make ethical decisions, I shouldn't focus on what anyone else is doing.

- I need to stay for my clients. If I leave, they won't have anyone who cares about their well-being.

- I'll just wait and see if things change in a month or so. If it's still this bad, I'll leave.

Acceptance

- I am doing my part to be a good therapist, but I need to be part of a system that fosters, supports, and respects good therapists.

- I accept that I deserve to feel respected in the workplace.

- I accept that this company probably won't change their policies.

- I accept the need to change my environment.

I understand that leaving a job feels scary. But therapists need to know when to stand for what's right. We chose careers that value ethics and prosocial change. We advocate tirelessly for our clients. But advocacy extends beyond the microsystem and beyond individual client care. Have you ever heard the metaphor about rearranging the deck chairs on the *Titanic*? If we're working on a sinking ship, we're a part of the problem.

Is It Internal Burnout, External Burnout, or Both?

When we talk about burnout, we must distinguish the type. Both types overlap, but the signs, symptoms, and treatment considerations differ.

Internal Burnout	External Burnout
A personal state characterized by exhaustion, cynicism, and a reduced sense of internal accomplishment	A personal state characterized by persistent external circumstances that impact professional functioning
Most common causes	Most common causes
<ul><li>Unrealistic expectations to control client outcomes</li><li>People-pleasing tendencies</li><li>Lack of boundaries between professional and personal life</li><li>Lack of self-care</li><li>Problems/crises in your personal life that impact your emotional well-being</li><li>Specializing in high-risk populations</li></ul>	<ul><li>Toxic work environment</li><li>Strong clashing of personalities between you and your supervisor or other colleagues</li><li>Lack or limited opportunity for workplace growth</li><li>Low wages</li><li>Jaded attitude about your company</li><li>Specializing in high-risk populations</li></ul>

Signs & Symptoms	Signs & Symptoms
• Depressed mood	• Dreading work
• Strained interpersonal relationships	• Resentment toward your supervisor, director, or colleagues
• Perpetual existential crises	• Procrastinating on essential work tasks
• Increased escape behaviors	
• Anxiety	• Dreading sessions with clients
• Questioning your career	• Loss of respect for company
• Irritability	• Questioning your career
• Apathy	• Taking more shortcuts in your work
• Compassion fatigue	
• Boredom in sessions	• Chronically feeling underappreciated or disrespected

Treatment Considerations	Treatment Considerations
• Seeking personal therapy	• Working with a new supervisor
• Reexamining and implementing more self-care	• Discussing your concerns with management
• Shifting more of a focus onto your physical well-being	• Changing roles within the company
• Pursuing different professional opportunities (attending trainings, reading new books)	• Seeking outside consultation or supervision
	• Strengthening your relationships with colleagues
• Taking a break from your career	• Leaving the company altogether

Coping with Internal Burnout: Why We Have Self-Care All Wrong

The concept of self-care has become so popular in recent years, and I appreciate the trend. We all need to value ourselves and practice more internal love and compassion. We all benefit from honoring our emotional health.

But self-care isn't just another item on our to-do list. It's so much more than a bubble bath or a brisk walk around the block. Self-care is a mindset, and it's one that most of us can work to improve.

Understand the Foundation of Compassion Fatigue

Compassion fatigue stems from our sincere desire to *give, give, give.* As therapists, we give endless patience and time and energy to our clients. We offer our calm and collected spirits for hours a day. But all this giving takes a toll, and good therapy isn't just about giving. Good therapy includes a balance of sharing and observing and analyzing and, at times, stepping back.

Distinguishing What's in Your Control

Despite what we give, we can control only ourselves. We can control our presence, reactions, and interventions. We can control arriving to work on time and sharing our struggles in supervision. We can control the room temperature and the way we arrange our decorative couch pillows. If we work in private practice, we can control our fees and the words used in our upbeat voicemail message. We can control what we choose to treat and whom we choose to treat.

Distinguishing What Isn't in Your Control

No matter who we are and what we offer, we can't control our clients. At all. Not even a little. We can't control their reactions, interpretations, or how they integrate the expert information we provide them. We can't control how they feel about us—whether they love, hate, or fear us. We have no say in which emotions they feel or don't feel. We also can't control if our coworkers speak too loudly or if an accident on the highway makes us late to work. We can't control whether someone clogs the only toilet in the communal bathroom or if a client throws a stapler at our head.

Accepting What Isn't in Your Control

When asked, most of us can distinguish what's not in our control. However, we rarely reflect on this mindset when meeting with clients. Instead, we can become frustrated and exhausted when our clients don't seem to get better. We can feel humiliated when we spend hours helping someone, only for them to find another therapist. We can feel angry when our colleague undermines us in a meeting. Over time, these feelings become overwhelming. We may lose the desire to give when we don't feel appreciated for our giving.

We must commit to being actively mindful about what isn't in our control. Of course, this is mostly everything. As I write this section, we're in the middle of the global COVID-19 pandemic. A few months ago, people waited in long lines at crowded restaurants and danced in sweaty nightclubs. Now, we're videoconferencing with family members and hoarding hand sanitizer. Who knows what the future will bring?

We don't have to like or support something to accept it. I don't like that a deadly virus has disrupted my daily life. I don't like when clients feel hopeless. I don't like when my baby decides to scream in the middle of the night instead of sleep. Acceptance just means that I understand the current reality, and I can't change it. I can allow myself to feel whatever I need to feel without judging the process.

The next time you feel overwhelmed or lost or otherwise emotionally exhausted, ask yourself what you're willing to release. Can you release the expectation that your client does her homework? The fear that your supervisor finds you incompetent? The disappointment that your roommate ate the last slice of pizza?

The less we tether ourselves to our emotions and our circumstances, the freer we feel. And the freer we feel, the lighter we are in our therapy sessions.

Respect That Self-Care May Change Over Time

In high school, I loved running. It made me feel strong and accomplished. Nothing beat the euphoria associated with the high I felt after finishing a long, hard run. I ran all throughout my city, through the nearby parks and beaches and mountains, and on vacations. I ran through sickness and in health. So many hours spent pounding the pavement, so many hours spent processing relationships and goals and traumas and all the other milestones we endure in this lifetime. I never thought I wouldn't run.

By the end of college, my days were filled with classes, studying, applying to graduate programs, working, and interning. In my limited free time, I wanted to hang out with my friends. Running became less important, but I still went out a few times each week. During these runs, I began feeling increasingly antsy. I scaled back on the distance and took more shortcuts. Sometimes, I (gasp!) skipped planned runs altogether. I had begun taking a yoga class with a friend, and I enjoyed it. My boyfriend at the time lifted weights, and I liked doing that, too.

But this evolution disturbed me. I was a runner! I convinced myself that I just needed more motivation. So I read some inspiring books and blogs about running. I followed a bunch of runners on social media. I bought new shoes and signed up for another half-marathon. I set my alarm each morning, but then I went an entire week hitting the snooze button.

I no longer wanted to run.

Unfortunately, we often struggle with letting go of identities, even when they no longer serve us. We think we need to commit to something forever. We associate changing our minds with giving up, and we associate giving up with weakness.

I'm no longer a runner. I've released this identity, although it took a while. At times, I see people jogging through my neighborhood, and I wistfully consider getting back into it. But these considerations are fleeting. I know the opportunity to run is there if I want.

We're allowed to release identities. We can change our relationships. We can find new hobbies. We can redefine who we are as people. Part of self-care is acknowledging what we really need, rather than what we think we're *supposed* to need.

Self-care changes because we change. We may have children, and our priorities shift. We may give up running, but we decide to try rock climbing (which I did!). We might enjoy CBT therapy, but Gestalt interests us, too.

Life changes constantly. We decide we want a divorce from our spouse. We realize we no longer believe in God. We decide to move to a different country. These changes are listed in no order of importance.

Then, sometimes, we change our minds again. And again. Be open to trying new things. Be open to your own growth.

Discipline Your Self-Care

Many people neglect self-care because they wait to be motivated or inspired to do it. But we need self-care the most when we feel the least inspired. When we're depressed and anxious, we don't necessarily want to practice deep breathing exercises or write a gratitude list. Instead, we often want to wallow in our discomfort or numb our feelings altogether.

When we don't practice self-care regularly, we need to discipline ourselves to commit to the process. I like weekly goals. Weeks offer a perfect, bite-sized experiment for self-care—weeks are more manageable than months, but they require more grit and commitment than days.

I recently committed to set a new self-care goal every week for a year. I made this chart for myself, and I keep track of my weekly assessments in a Google Doc.

Weekly Self-Care Goal Assessment

Date	May 20, 2020
Identified goal	I will meditate for 10 minutes each morning this week.
Why I am setting this goal	I want to increase my daily mindfulness. I feel restful when I meditate. I know meditation has many positive benefits.
How I plan to achieve this goal	I will set a timer on my phone and meditate after brushing my teeth and before I take a shower each morning. I will tell my husband about my goal so he knows to not disturb me.
Any identified obstacles	If I'm running late that morning, I might be tempted to skip it. If my baby is crying, I will probably feel the need to stop the meditation practice. I might try to push it off until later in the afternoon or evening.
Did I complete the goal?	Yes
How challenging was it to complete this goal? (0-10)	5

If I didn't complete the goal, what prevented me from doing so?	N/A: Completed
If I did, what difference did it make in my well-being this week?	I felt a little more rested and peaceful in the morning. I noticed myself more present for the hour or so after meditating.
If applicable, what edits would I make to this goal in the future?	I would like to meditate for 15 minutes daily. 10 minutes didn't feel long enough for me to really connect with the moment.

Here are my observations from doing this activity over the past few months:

- When I write something down, it makes it real.

- I'm competitive with myself. I don't like the idea of not completing a goal.

- I don't always know what's going to be challenging. Some goals, like meditating for a few minutes each day, sound easy at first, but they become challenging as the week goes on.

- I can do almost anything for seven days.

If you struggle with self-care, I invite you to try my assessment model for three months and reevaluate. We all know that self-care is a process. One week of perfect self-care doesn't mean much if you neglect yourself the rest of the time. Be consistent, hold yourself accountable, and remind yourself that you deserve to do this.

Assess Your Drug and Alcohol Consumption

Many therapists dance a fine line between using substances as "self-care" and being at risk for a legitimate substance use disorder. If you have an actual problem, you will tempt this line over and over again. You will disregard it, cross it, redraw it, and you will also pretend it doesn't exist. Then you will hastily point to your job, family, and academics, and convince yourself that you're functioning *just fine.*

We use drugs and alcohol for a variety of reasons. First, they feel good. They activate all those enticing hormones like dopamine, serotonin, and norepinephrine, which help us feel pleasure and provide a means to temporarily escape our life circumstances. And our life circumstances are stressful! We're sleep-deprived. We're depressed. We're anxious. We're doubting our choices. Work sucks. Our family sucks even more. And so we get drunk or high, and we justify the pattern.

Substance abuse is insidious and unforgiving. It also tends to progress. I've worked with many fantastic therapists who lost significant footing because of their drug or alcohol consumption. It's sad, and it's also scary. You can jeopardize your reputation and destroy your health. You can ruin your career before it even starts.

If you have a substance abuse problem, despite what your soul-crushing shame may tell you, you are not a failure. You do, however, need help. If you even think you struggle with addictive tendencies, now is the time for intervention. Even if you're not sure. Even if you work full-time and take care of seven ferrets and drink only light beer. Even if you tell yourself you could probably stop if you really wanted to stop.

At best, disregarding your addiction can easily make you a distracted or ineffective therapist. At worst, you risk decimating your physical and emotional well-being.

Do Not Play Therapist to People Who Are Not Your Clients

Your friends are not your clients.

Your mother is not your client.

Your neighbor's aunt's turtle is not your client.

People find therapists fascinating, and they can and will solicit us for advice. Often, once someone discovers our career, they love to ask if we can read their mind or if we're analyzing their every move. Then, they will say something like, "Since you're a therapist, I was just wondering..."

Unfortunately, many therapists tumble into these sneaky traps. We give our Uber drivers pointers for setting boundaries with their roommates. We advise our hairstylists on grounding techniques to use during a panic attack. Our best friends call us begging for advice, and they dazzle us with the charming line, "You can practice being a therapist with me!"

Of course, we should respect, listen, and love people deeply and wholeheartedly. We can be empathic and unconditionally supportive of their struggles. If they ask us for direct advice, we can offer it. But we must also know the key differences between being good friends and professional therapists.

Healthy relationships maintain a mutual symbiosis of giving and receiving. The boundaries are respected, and the scale feels mostly balanced. Both parties can lean on each other in times of need. That said, many therapists fall into the trap of being the only giver in their relationships. Just like with their clients, they withhold their needs and expectations. They cater to the other person. They fall into the endless cycle of listening, doling out empathy, and forever rescuing friends from excruciating Tinder dates. If this is your pattern, you must reevaluate how you seek connection.

Many therapists have an unhealthy desire to feel needed. This need gives us validation and power. We help others feel better—we're so special and talented that people spend their money and time, and share their vulnerability with us! This unique authority can feel seductive, especially for therapists struggling with low self-esteem.

But what happens when we play the therapist in our personal lives? We foster codependent dynamics where people rely on us for free support and validation. We gravitate toward needy people who only want to take from us. We solidify our rigid roles as caretakers or givers.

Set limits for yourself, and set limits with your family and friends. They are not your clients.

Maintain Friendships with People Who Aren't Therapists

Therapists are such a special breed, aren't we? We are painfully intense. We feel, think, and experience the world in profound and mystical ways. We analyze everything, and then we analyze it three more times to make sure we didn't miss any details.

How can you tell you're on a date with a therapist? They talk about their childhood trauma in the first ten minutes. We love depth, and we move into it quickly. We value the raw and vulnerable parts of self-expression. Our biggest pet peeve is small talk; we abhor it like we abhor loud, obnoxious neighbors or sluggish Internet connections.

We are, at times, nauseating.

We crave soul work, and we're quick to discard anything that doesn't fit in that box. It's no surprise that some of my closest friends are mental health professionals. They speak my language. They understand the strange and complicated details of what I do for a living because they're also doing it. There's no need to explain the awkwardness of erotic transference or the pain associated with a premature termination. They've been there, they get it, and they are eager to swap their own clinical war stories with me.

But here's what can happen when we only spend free time with other therapists. First, we can lose ourselves in a bottomless pit of solely thinking and talking about work. At the beginning of our careers, this concern rarely fazes us. After all, whenever we start a new chapter in our lives, we feel captivated by it. We don't mind if it consumes all of our attention because we become enmeshed with the work. It becomes an extension of who we are and what we do.

Years later, the compounded impact of revolving everything around work makes us boring conversationalists. It can also contribute to burnout, as we have no real way of separating our professional identities from our social ones.

We can talk with some people about our pasts and the meaning of the universe and how our mothers failed as a secure base. But we should also maintain relationships that don't depend on this constant enthralling and deep conversation.

It's healthy to have lighter relationships and friends who don't require soul work. These people can help us recharge—they can remind us that life doesn't always need to be so serious.

Maximize Your Flow Time

The best moments in our lives are not the passive, receptive, relaxing times...The best moments usually occur if a person's body or mind is stretched to its limits in a voluntary effort to accomplish something difficult and worthwhile. —Mihaly Csikszentmihalyi, PhD

Many people associate self-care with relaxation. When we talk about self-care, we talk about getting pedicures or watching funny videos on YouTube. Embracing relaxation feels good, and it can foster our well-being.

But excess leisure can backfire. Have you ever spent eight hours watching television reruns? Have you ever spent an entire week lounging on a tropical beach doing nothing but drinking daiquiris and eating tacos? Because I have.

At first, there's this amazing sense of contentment. Sinking into the relaxation allows us to release the tension we carry. But I notice when I gorge on leisure, I quickly become lethargic. And although we often use relaxation to combat feeling depressed or anxious, too much relaxation can exacerbate the negative emotions.

Some therapists don't want to use their brains outside of work hours. This mindset is understandable. They often feel so exhausted by the end of the day that they can't think beyond their desire to zone out. But what if we shifted zoning out to zoning in? Because once we learn how to zone in to the right space, we can restore some of our energy and find the fulfillment we crave.

Getting in the Zone

Mihaly Csikszentmihalyi, PhD coined the concept of flow to describe the feeling we experience during total immersion in a task or activity. When we're in flow, we're in the zone. We feel entirely focused on the current task. We don't worry about the time. We don't think about the laundry or tonight's dinner plans. We are operating in the moment, fully present and absorbed. Csikszentmihalyi indicates that flow requires seven conditions:

- **Immersion:** You're fully present and focused on what you're doing.

- **Sense of ecstasy:** In Greek, ecstasy refers to standing outside of something. In other words, you've stepped outside your normal reality. You're so engaged in this new reality that you can't tell if you're hungry or tired.

- **Greater inner clarity:** You know what you need to keep doing—the tasks are laid out in front of you. You move through them seamlessly.

- **Doable:** You believe you have adequate skills to achieve the tasks. They may be challenging, but they're not so challenging that you feel discouraged.

- **Sense of serenity:** The ego is removed, and you aren't worried about yourself. You feel a sense of humility about the work.

- **Timelessness:** Time seems irrelevant. Entire hours may pass without you realizing it.

- **Intrinsic motivation:** Instead of a desired end result, the flow itself is the actual reward. Everything else is an added benefit.

Ideally, we experience flow in some of our therapy sessions. I know that I experience it when meeting with some of my favorite clients. In those sessions, I feel focused and attuned. Even if I feel challenged,

I also feel excited and engaged. The hour often moves quickly. I am in sync with my client, and I feel confident in what I'm doing. The process seems fluid—I trust it, and I trust myself.

However, we can't expect to meet all of our flow needs while at work. That places far too much emphasis on our careers. We also need to experience flow in our personal lives. That will keep us eager and happy and driven outside of our therapist identities. Consider trying these flow-based activities:

- Any physical sport
- Making art (photography, sculpting, painting, pottery, needlework, scrapbooking)
- Writing
- Music (playing instruments, writing songs, singing)
- DIY projects or chores
- Playing games
- Cooking and baking
- Working with animals

Flow is action-based, and it requires effort, discipline, and actual work. You must invest time to learn new skills, and you need to commit to practice.

Flow does use your brain. It just uses your brain in a way that recharges—rather than depletes—your energy.

Seek Awe Often

The most beautiful thing we can experience is the mysterious. It is the source of all true art and all science. He to whom this emotion is a stranger, who can no longer pause to wonder and stand rapt in awe, is as good as dead: his eyes are closed. -Albert Einstein

Just like we struggle to understand self-care, we also struggle to understand happiness. We crave it, but we don't quite know how to find and hold on to the feeling. Instead, we often jump on hedonistic treadmills and buy new shoes and cars because we believe that's going to be the thing that brings us pleasure.

I stumbled upon Dacher Keltner, PhD a few years ago. At the time, I was struggling with depression, and I wanted to learn more about happiness. In his research, Keltner discovered that awe—above other emotions—encourages people to sacrifice, cooperate, and share resources with others. When we feel awe, we also experience a greater sense of abundance and self-compassion. Additionally, it sharpens our minds helps us to think more critically.

But my favorite part of awe is that awe helps us feel small and insignificant. At first, this may seem strange. Why would we want to feel small and insignificant? Aren't we super important? Isn't happiness supposed to be about feeling good within ourselves?

Actually, no. We're not all that important. That big mistake we thought we made isn't that important, either. When we consider the sheer volume of people and life and all the other intricate systems that keep our universe in working order, we're just mere, microscopic specs. We hardly matter. And when we realize that, we become more humble.

Humbleness has a prosocial effect. It fosters empathy—it evens out the emotional playing field with other people. We see other people's needs as important. Therefore, we tend to act more kindly and modestly. Humbleness also corresponds with gratitude. They reinforce each other. When we feel grateful, we want to share and give to the people around us. And when we give to the people around us, we make the world a better place. Everyone wins.

Humbleness also keeps our problems in perspective. Burnout in our professional work usually results from our desire to control. We want to fix, save, and change our clients. We take our jobs so seriously. Humbleness acts as a catalyst in keeping the larger picture of our lives in focus.

We can experience awe in different ways. Nature gives me awe. There is something so profoundly indescribable about how the universe has created all these magnificent trees and mountains and ecosystems. I feel awe when I gaze up at the stars. The nighttime sky reminds me that I'm not the center of the universe, and I frequently need that reminder. Some other ways to induce awe include:

- watching inspiring movies or documentaries.

- listening to music that sings to your entire soul.

- visiting an art gallery or museum.

- traveling to famous monuments or national parks.

- listening to a thought-provoking speech or discussion.

- taking a mindful walk to enjoy the sights, sounds, and sensations.

Remember That Your Time Has Monetary Value

In my adult life, I spent many years debating about hiring a professional cleaning service. I wanted the help, but the expense felt extravagant and inappropriate. I knew how to turn on my Roomba. I could wipe down a countertop and scrub grime. To compound the debate, I also had rigid beliefs about what it meant to hire a cleaning service. I assumed only very wealthy or lazy people did it. And as a responsible and capable (and not wealthy) adult, I could take care of my own home.

And then I had a baby.

Like most new parents, before giving birth, I had hopelessly unrealistic visions of motherhood. My life wasn't going to change all that much—I'd just strap him into his baby carrier and take him wherever I went. At home, we'd play together until he grew tired. Then I'd put him down for a nap, and he'd sleep peacefully for two hours. I would use that time to clean the house, take care of my work, and even meditate!

If you're a mother, you know exactly how this story unfolds. Newborns don't exactly play. They cry, eat, and poop. The sleeping, if it happens at all, is rarely peaceful, especially in those first months. And nothing productive gets done.

Before our son was born, my husband's boss gifted us with a month's worth of professional cleaning services. If you ever want to give a new parent the best gift in the history of baby gifts, skip the stroller and diapers. That's the gift to give.

The crew arrived. They worked three times faster than I did, and they did the job three times better. We've been getting our house cleaned ever since.

Time is the only resource we can't replenish. It's finite. Once the minute passes, it's gone forever. After a year concludes, it's done. We can't get any of it back. That second you spent reading that sentence is gone, and now you're one second closer to your death. Let that *really* sink in. Let it sink in so much that it scares you.

Over the years, I've had to give myself permission to value my time. It's not free. In fact, it's become more and more valuable as I've gotten older and grown in my career and wealth.

How Do You Really Put a Number on the Value of Time?

Of course, everyone's monetary value of time is different. This number isn't arbitrary—it changes based on individual needs and life circumstances. You need to discover what yours is. This figure doesn't need to be rigid, but you should have an idea of what an hour means to you. Play around with that number until it feels right. If you search online, several quizzes can help you with this calculation. They'll assess your current salary and ask questions about how much you're willing to spend on certain services.

We all have the same twenty-four hours in a day. You, me, the Dalai Lama, Beyonce. No matter how wealthy you are, you don't get to buy more time. But when you start monetizing your hours, you inherently prioritize what matters.

Time matters. Life is fast and it's fleeting, and that should scare you enough to want to honor and respect it.

Allow Yourself to Ask for Help

I struggled in my first few months of being a new mother. Like many women, I believed I needed to do everything myself. After all, I wanted and planned for my child, and I told myself I knew the investment that parenting required. I associated asking for help with weakness, with being incompetent and inferior.

These issues often first emerge in childhood. Many of us are raised to think and act independently. We believe asking for help means depending on other people, which makes us feel inadequate. Therefore, we want to figure things out on our own. We don't want to burden other people. We don't want to owe anyone anything. And so, we resist advice and support, and we never, ever want to hear those dreaded words, I told you so!

The road to vulnerability recovery is treacherous. I can't pretend I'm anywhere close to a finish line because I still have so much work to do. Not only do I struggle to ask for help, but I also struggle to accept the help after I've asked for it! This issue comes from a shame-based place of believing that others will find me annoying or incapable if I need support. That voice says I don't deserve the support.

But we are social creatures. We are designed to work in teams, designed to lift and mentor and lean on one another. We work best when we work together. When we try to do everything ourselves, we become overwhelmed and depressed. We become resentful. Additionally, our foolproof method isn't foolproof at all. When we're too busy, things invariably fall through the cracks. And when we notice whatever fell through the cracks, we feel more ashamed, frustrated, and anxious. But instead of stepping back and acknowledging that we've spread ourselves too thin, we insist we need to organize ourselves better and focus more. We just need to work harder. The self-shaming cycle ensues.

Admitting When You Need Help in Your Career

Many therapists like to pretend they have everything under control. We might feel safe venting to our coworkers about our insecurities, but we often fail to acknowledge when we need help. We don't want our teachers, supervisors, or bosses to doubt our capabilities. But we all face hardships in this career. We all struggle with certain protocols or clients or structural issues. Signs you need help in your career include:

- constantly feeling anxious about work.

- believing you're on the brink of getting fired.

- feeling lost with your clients.

- thinking you messed up in a session but not feeling sure what to do next.

- feeling constantly exhausted, overwhelmed, or irritated by your clients.

Find Strength in Humor

Comedians use humor to highlight the nuances of everyday life. They tell colorful stories, and they infuse joy into bleak situations. When done well, their humor unifies their audience. It creates a shared experience of connection.

Some therapists and clients find my Psychotherapy Memes content offensive. I know this because I often receive messages telling me how insensitive and cruel I am. I understand why they might think this way. My humor is sarcastic, self-deprecating, and it's dark. At times, it can seem mean. Additionally, most people have a strange relationship with this kind of humor—they feel ashamed laughing at something that's supposed to be serious.

Yet humor helps us survive. While memes are a recent phenomenon, commiserating about work isn't. People mingle in one another's offices to vent about their day. They linger over happy hour margaritas to share their troubles. They complain to their spouses when they return home from work. Dark humor and sarcasm aren't new, but now we can use the Internet to share it more freely and globally.

I like to laugh at myself. I like to laugh with my clients. I also like to laugh with my coworkers. I don't hide this from anyone. Life is hard, and laughter makes it easier. Therapists aren't infallible. We don't need to be so stiff and impersonal. Humor makes something real. It gives it texture and life.

Of course, I don't believe in laughing at clients. That's not what humor is about. Humor isn't about hurting or ostracizing people. We don't tell jokes at the expense of someone else's feelings. And therapy is sacred; it deserves our respect and merit. But we're all humans. Life is weird, and we don't need to feel so alone in our experiences. We're allowed to laugh, and laughter is a crucial ingredient in our self-care recipes.

CHAPTER 9:

HOW TO BE A THERAPIST IN THE MODERN WORLD

In this final chapter, I address some common issues that modern therapists face. I'm not pretending to have all the answers. I'm only going to say my piece.

Understand That School (Probably) Won't Teach You About Business

I made my first business plan in a journal decorated with faded unicorn stickers. I was six years old and selling Girl Scout cookies. Unlike my simple-minded peers, I didn't just want to smile and knock on doors asking neighbors if they wanted my product. I wanted to sell, and I wanted to be the top seller in my troop.

To accomplish my lofty goal, I paid attention to people's behaviors. First, I realized that more people bought cookies after eating dinner than in the morning or afternoon. That was when their resolve went down, fatigue went up, and gorging on sugar apparently fixed all the problems of the day. I also noticed that my older neighbors purchased more cookies than the younger neighbors. However, there was a trade-off for their generous investment. They often wanted to spend more time interacting with me—they liked to ask questions about my troop and school. And since I was at the mercy of my parents' time, time wasn't a resource I could waste.

I noted all these crucial trends in my dedicated journal. I kept track of my neighbors, their orders, and how I could get them to order more boxes. Yes, I was six. Yes, I was weird.

This entrepreneurial spirit carried me throughout adolescence and early adulthood. Over the years, the hustles and ventures have varied. I've bought and flipped used items to make a profit. I've written resumes. I've tested products and written descriptions for them. My husband and I owned a successful business selling succulent planters (not a joke).

What's the secret behind my entrepreneurial success? The secret is that there isn't a secret. It doesn't lie in hustling Thin Mints. It doesn't lie in overpriced masterclasses or single tricks promising to land you millions of dollars. The secret lies in the seemingly dull combination of talent, effort, intense grit, and some luck. It also lies in paying attention to details and in noting that your older neighbors buy more cookies than your younger ones.

Many therapists struggle with the business side of the work. They feel guilty charging money for their services. They feel overwhelmed by marketing and advertising their skills. As a result, their businesses fail miserably. Let's review some common business setbacks and how to cope with them.

Fear

We all know how fear works. We need some of it to survive. Without fear, we would touch hot ovens and get eaten by bears. Fear keeps us in check; it reminds us that we're fallible humans who need to be cautious and aware of our surroundings.

But fear can have its downside. Unprocessed fear leaves us feeling timid and guarded. It prevents us from embracing vulnerability, and it can keep us from taking necessary risks. The common fears associated with private practice include:

- Fear of getting started in the first place
- Fear of obtaining clients
- Fear of retaining clients
- Fear of missed opportunities elsewhere
- Fear of financial insecurity
- Fear of liability with your clients

If you're struggling with fear, I recommend identifying the bullet point that stands out to you the most. Work on that one first. Sit with it, play with it, explore it in your own therapy or with colleagues or with journaling, or all of the above.

What would change if you didn't have that fear? How is that fear keeping you stuck? What do you need to do about it?

Lack of a Solid Business Plan

Many therapists start their own practice because it seems like the best thing to do. They grow tired of agency work, desire more money, or want greater control over their clients and caseloads. But in business, knowing why you want to do something isn't nearly as important as knowing how you intend to do it.

You might succeed without a business plan, but I wouldn't count on it. To achieve your goals, you need structure and intention. You need to understand market trends and how they correspond with your ideal clients.

In my content marketing business, I work with many therapists launching their private-practice websites. When we first start collaborating, I help them narrow down their vision of their dream practice. What kind of clients do they want to see? How old are the clients, and what are the types of presenting problems? What are the therapist's likes and dislikes? What articles would prospective clients be most interested in reading? And most of all, why should anyone choose them to help solve their problems? If you can't answer these questions, you won't know how to market your practice efficiently.

Like treatment plans, business plans keep entrepreneurs organized and efficient. Therapists who wish to start a private practice need a foundation to establish their goals, and business plans concretize loose ideas. This process is psychologically important. When we take our ventures seriously, we're more likely to demand others do as well.

I always recommend making a business plan before you even start the transition into private practice. There are many free templates available online. Some of them are simple; others are extremely lengthy and thorough. Regardless of the template, your plan should include the following items:

- **Executive summary:** This is the overall summary of your business. It should include your business name, location, the types of services you offer, and your mission statement.

- **Services and products:** What do you intend to provide for your clients, and how much will each of these things cost?

- **Market analysis and strategy:** Who is in your target demographic, and how do you intend to reach those clients? Who are your competitors, and what are their strengths and weaknesses? What's the need for additional services? What are the current trends in your area? What doesn't exist that you can offer?

- **Financial information:** How much will it cost for you to operate? How will your business stay afloat each month? What kind of costs do you anticipate encountering? What do you estimate your growth will be? Do you need to meet with an accountant?

- **Legal information:** What types of insurance do you need? What contracts or licenses need to be in place before you get started? Do you need to consult with an attorney?

- **Operational plan:** How will you keep your business running? Where will your office be located? What hours will you work? If you plan on hiring additional staff, what will be their roles? What third-party services do you intend to use?

If you feel overwhelmed by answering all these questions, that's a good thing. It means you're getting a realistic feel for the challenges associated with running a business. It's better to feel overwhelmed before seeing clients than feel completely lost a few months after starting.

I also recommend dedicating a few months to learn the ins and outs of business in general. I contacted therapists working in private practice and asked them questions. I also joined Facebook groups for therapists. I talked with my accountant, and I also consulted with a lawyer. I spent time working on a business plan, and I revised that plan often. But, above all, I focused on building connections—even if you're working alone, don't go at it alone.

Oversaturated Market

Oversaturated markets can be intimidating for new therapists. What can help you stand out from the other therapists in your local area? How do you intend to get prospective clients into your office? If you plan to work with cash-pay clients, how do you justify your rate?

Therapists on health insurance panels often receive more client referrals than those who try to solicit business independently. Some therapists prefer this option. There is a greater sense of financial stability and less pressure to market oneself. However, insurance reimbursement entails more paperwork, billing, and (usually) lower pay. You must comply with each insurance company's guidelines for therapy. Navigating these guidelines can be challenging.

Having a niche often helps therapists find their footing in oversaturated markets. But you don't need to limit your niche to a single diagnosis. A niche can include a specific population, theoretical orientation, and your own cultural identity (i.e., some clients want a therapist with a particular religious affiliation or ethnicity). Therapists often fear that a niche can be too restrictive. However, by specializing your focus, you can better target your marketing, networking, and continuing education.

"I'm My Own Boss" Mentality

Being your own boss has its obvious advantages. Nobody is micromanaging your work or forcing you to follow asinine rules. You can make your own decisions, and you have total control over the business operations. There's also more opportunity for financial and personal growth—you can set your rates and choose the services you offer.

But all freedoms come with expensive costs, and this cost won't be worth it for everyone. When you don't have a designated boss, the clients are your bosses. Without them, there is no business, and there is no pay. They determine whether you can pay rent that month. Your reputation is of the utmost importance, and you need to do everything you can to preserve it.

To succeed, you need to be willing to take risks, sacrifice your time, and brave through the storms of uncertainty. There's nobody else keeping you accountable. It's just you and your level of commitment. Think about this before you start.

In Private Practice, Your Website Is Your Storefront

In every profession, word-of-mouth referrals are the cheapest (and most effective) form of marketing. But therapists cannot rely on this funnel alone. You need a website. An *amazing* website. It's not enough to have a few stock photos and generic lines of text. You need an eye-popping website that captures who you are as a therapist.

In my business, I help professionals build their online presence. Having a bad website—even more than having no website—tends to be the greatest detriment to their business. I strongly urge you to hire a dedicated professional for this task. You wouldn't build your own store if you didn't understand construction. Don't build your own website if you don't understand coding and design. If you've ever heard the term SEO, don't gloss over that, either. SEO stands for search engine optimization, and implementing it into your site successfully drives you to Google's first pages. SEO is technical and complicated, consisting of many components: keywords, meta descriptions, backlinks, on-site optimization, site performance, internal linking, external linking, social bookmarking, content...am I overwhelming you yet?

Again, I recommend you hire a professional to help you manage this work. If you want to succeed as a therapist in the modern world, you must open every avenue for success. And most prospective clients are going to start their search online. You want to make sure they can find you!

No Matter Where You Work, Everything You Share Online Is Fair Game

I give this suggestion as someone who has built an anonymous community through satirical memes.

I went back and forth in deciding if I should publish this book under my real name. My personal life, professional life, and meme-making life are all very different from one another. I worried about therapists and clients assuming my crass attitude meant I didn't care about the work. I also considered the potential liability. If I offended someone or accidentally provided inaccurate information, could I be sued? Could my reputation be destroyed?

Ultimately, I decided to publish this book under my real name because I felt ready to own up to my work, even if it meant dealing with some backlash. I also hope that revealing my name will inadvertently advance my career, both as a therapist and writer. I know the risks, and while they scare me, I have chosen to accept them.

That said, I do urge that you double-check *everything* you post on online. You need to know what people can see when they search your name. Clients, colleagues, and potential bosses will absolutely check. They will plug your name into search engines, and some will look at everything posted about you. That blog article you published three years ago. That tagged photo of you drunk in Cancun. The LinkedIn profile you haven't updated since college.

And some will go further than that. They will look at your mother's dog and your husband's place of work, and they will view every item posted on your public wedding registry. Call it stalking, or call it research, but if it's available to the public, people can consume it.

Online Recommendations

- If you have personal social media pages, set them all to private. Do not allow people to tag you in pictures or posts without your approval.

- Consider using a different name or nickname for your social media pages.

- If you maintain public social media pages for your practice, always assume that your current or prospective clients will see everything you post.

- Have a LinkedIn and personal website (especially if you're in private practice). In our increasingly digital world, most clients and employers want to be able to find *something* about you.

Therapy Will Continue to Evolve

Therapy continues to become more popular and mainstream. But it's changed rapidly in recent years. Short-term, cognitive models are becoming the norm. More clients are gravitating toward telehealth options. At the time of this writing, BetterHelp, the largest online therapy platform, advertises that its services have helped over two million people. Additionally, since the passing of the Affordable Care Act in 2010, many people now use their insurance to pay for some or all of their treatment.

The way we understand and treat mental illness also continues to evolve. The American Psychiatric Association only removed the diagnosis of homosexuality from the DSM in 1973. In the past decade, we've since added diagnoses like hoarding disorder, excoriation, binge-eating disorder, and genito-pelvic pain/penetration disorder. Each DSM update revises our perceptions of mental illness.

I suspect we'll make tremendous strides in both artificial intelligence and psychotropic medications in the coming years. I think we'll see more movement toward virtual reality, and I imagine online therapy will continue to rise in popularity. These shifts will change the nature of treatment. Furthermore, I suspect that, in a few hundred years, therapists will look back at our current methods and deem many of them faulty or downright barbaric.

There's no place for stagnation in this field. I understand that some of us value the "heart" part of therapy. I'm one of those people. I like the old-school, face-to-face, bare-your-entire-soul-to-me type of therapy. That therapy will always be needed. But we also must be realistic and show a willingness to adapt when adaptation is required.

Closing Thoughts: Remember Why You Started

Good therapy is as challenging as it is beautiful. Day in and day out, we unpack pain and process fear and sew together the broken pieces of souls, hearts, and trust. We battle with defense mechanisms. We hold tears and fears and everything in between.

We never really know what happens to most of our clients after they leave our office for the last time. We never really know if we did the right thing or said the right thing.

We give so much.

We are imperfect. We are completely and utterly imperfect. And that's what makes us so wonderful. We are human—we can empathize with our clients, and we can embrace the parallel process of vulnerability together.

Remember why you started.

Was it because you had a therapist who believed in you? Because you wanted to do your part in breaking the stigma about mental health? Because you wanted to make a difference?

This work will challenge you, stretch you, and make you question your values, goals, and livelihood. This work will hurt. Stay in the field long enough, and you'll understand what seasoned therapists mean when they say that you truly do hear everything.

Stay in this field long enough, and you'll come to believe that everybody on this planet feels pain.

In this work, you will meet all kinds of people. You will learn so many things. You will watch clients progress in ways you still need to progress. You will find yourself amazed at human resilience. We are so incredibly resilient.

Remember why you started.

Some clients will consume tremendous space in your mind. Their stories will linger with you for years. You will wonder about them in the middle of a conversation with someone else. They will emerge in your dreams. Some clients will make you feel profoundly sad that you couldn't be friends. You will have to remind yourself that this relationship is unique, unlike any other relationship in the world. At times, this will frustrate you.

You will watch shows and read books, and you will diagnose the characters. You will play surrogate therapist for your friends, even though I instructed you to avoid that. If you decide to have a baby, you will eliminate so many prospective names off your list because they'll remind you of past clients. If you're married to a therapist, like I am, this task will become even harder.

Your clients will teach you lessons, and their stories will transcend how you think about the inner workings of the mind. You will learn about love and how it stretches and collapses, and how it motivates every action we take. You will learn about fear and bravery and trauma, all of which our clients carry into the room. You will learn about suicide and psychosis and heroin and fetishes you didn't know existed. It will equally exhaust and inspire you.

Remember why you started.

You will learn in every session, and you will teach in every session. That is the stunning symbiosis of what we therapists do for our clients. That is why this relationship is so sacred. As flawed people, we grow together. Good therapy is breathless. Good therapy transcends a book, and good therapy transcends any cerebral explanation.

Remember why you started.

When you strip aside the interventions and the schooling and the textbooks, we are humans who listen and connect to other humans. We are masters of pain because we find peace with pain. And pain, even more than love, is the only universal human experience. But we get to help people heal from it. We matter.

Remember why you're here. You can do this. And beyond that, you can do this *well*.

ABOUT THE AUTHOR

Nicole Arzt is a psychotherapist, author, creator of Psychotherapy Memes, business owner, woman, wife, mother, travel fiend, coffee snob, and recovering perfectionist. These titles are listed in no real order of importance, but each of these roles has impacted the shaping of this book.

She lives in Southern California with her husband, son, and two rambunctious dogs. She's awkward, messy, and perpetually in at least four existential crises.

For questions, inquiries, or to schedule a press/media speaking, contact her at nicole.m.arzt@gmail.com.

REFERENCES

American Psychiatric Association. (2013). *Highlights of Changes from DSM-IV-TR to DSM-5*. American Psychiatric Publishing. https://www.psychiatry.msu.edu/_files/docs/Changes-From-DSM-IV-TR-to-DSM-5.pdf

Drescher, J. (2015). Out of DSM: Depathologizing Homosexuality. *Behavioral sciences (Basel, Switzerland)*, 5(4), 565–575. https://doi.org/10.3390/bs5040565

Kottler, J. (2010). *On Being a Therapist*. John Wiley & Sons, Inc.

Lord, N. (2017, June 5). *That Time Sigmund Freud Nearly Killed a Patient- and Then Got Hooked on Cocaine*. Narratively. https://narratively.com/when-sigmund-freud-got-hooked-on-cocaine/

Puder, D. (2019). *Episode 041: What is Transference and Countertransference?* https://static1.squarespace.com/static/5ef3b2b2b1eee677b315048f/t/5f20a6033fc04b6c1726582e/1595975171368/041_Puder_What+is+Transference+and+Countertransference_.pdf

Winerman, L. (2011, October). *Suppressing the "white bears."* American Psychological Association. https://www.apa.org/monitor/2011/10/unwanted-thoughts

Yalom, I. (2002). *The Gift of Therapy: An Open Letter to a New Generation of Therapists and Their Patients*. HarperCollins Publishers.

9 781735 993508